STORIES OF FAMOUS EXPLORERS

STORIES OF FAMOUS EXPLORERS

LEONARD GRIBBLE

Illustrated by Elizabeth Hammond

ARTHUR BARKER LIMITED
20 New Bond Street London W1

Printed in Great Britain by
Bristol Typesetting Co. Ltd.
Barton Manor - St. Philips
Bristol 2

CONTENTS

CONTENTS

ILLUSTRATIONS

For any boy or girl from seven to seventy with an
itch to go out and find a new way to anywhere

AUTHOR'S PREFACE

F E W narratives are more stirring than stories of exploration, for they not only tell of man's conquest of the physical unknown confronting him, but relate how by free choice he journeyed into that hazardous unknown, determined to discover a great new truth or suffer defeat, often when to fail meant to perish.

Fortunately for the human race, most explorers of note have capped their curiosity and courage with notable discoveries, and in this book the purpose has been to show how, from earliest recorded times, a pattern of achievement has evolved over the successive centuries of exploration.

When that south-western Sea of Darkness chilled men's blood in an age of even darker superstition the maritime Venetians took to the land and out-journeyed the Arabs in their travel eastwards. When the Conquistadores sailed west Portuguese caravels voyaged east. When the Dutch sat in comfort on their East Indies verandas, hoarding the fragrant spices in their warehouses, the English roved south to occupy and colonize lands the Dutch had ignored, as they had sailed south and west and north from Europe when Mediterranean galleons were fanning out across the southern Atlantic. Not surprisingly the picaresque element finds its colourful place in all this activity. The buccaneers and privateers sailed towards those points of the compass that had trembled to the roar of cannon and clash of steel in the new worlds being explored and occupied.

Trade followed the flag, and upon occasion the flag followed trade. It was one or the other, with often no marked difference in the eventual outcome.

Yet in appraising the explorers it would be unfair not to acknowledge the impetus provided by the dreamer and the visionary who created the atmosphere in which men of action could achieve. Prince Henry never went to sea to explore, yet had he not lived the history of the past five centuries might have been vastly different.

Had not a Westminster schoolboy named Richard Hakluyt visited his cousin in the Middle Temple on a day when the lawyer host was in a mood to show him some ' books of cosmography with a universal map', Sir Humphrey Gilbert might never have founded the first English colony in Newfoundland and thereby started a process that, by democratic progression, has resulted in the establishing of more free nations in the mid-twentieth century than ever was carved by a conqueror's sword.

For it was the boy Hakluyt who, while listening to his cousin's voice as he ' pointed with his wand to all the known seas, gulfs, bays, straits, capes, rivers, empires, kingdoms, dukedoms, and territories of each part, with declaration also of their special commodities and particular wants, which by the benefit of traffic and enterprise of merchants are plentifully supplied', realized he had found a purpose in his young life and a mission to fulfil. This was no less than to awaken other Englishmen to the qualities and capacities of English captains and navigators who had been ' either ignominiously reported or exceedingly condemned', whereas those of other, less phlegmatic races had been ' miraculously extolled'.

Hakluyt the clerk in holy orders not only wrote his great *Voyages,* he actually journeyed to Bristol and argued with the port's worthies to ensure their support for Sir Humphrey Gilbert's new experiments in exploration and his fixed intention of making what were termed diligent inquiries that could ' yield unto our western discovery in America '.

Such men as Prince Henry and the Reverend Richard Hakluyt belong not only to their own nations, but to all mankind, as do the true explorers of the quality of da Gama and Magellan, Hudson and Cook, and more recently Amundsen and Livingstone.

Alexander, we are told, contented himself with sighing for new worlds to conquer. The astronauts of the second half of the twentieth century are speeding from their terrestrial background seeking paths to other worlds in outer space.

Perhaps the era of man's greatest exploration is about to dawn. If so, then certainly the explorers who find a place in the following pages have played their part in bequeathing to the descendants of their race all the bright tomorrows that are promised.

OUT OF THE MISTS

A R O U N D the year 1500 BC an incredible freighter was built on the banks of the Nile. It was constructed specially to convey two granite obelisks up the Egyptian river from the Temple of Hatshepsut at Karnak. Each obelisk was some hundred feet long and weighed about seven hundred tons. The ship that carried them was something of a wonder in its day. We know practically nothing about its construction, but it seems reasonable to suppose that most of the timber used by the shipwrights came from Berytus, one of the eight ports of the Phoenicians, stretching from Gaza to Aradus, on the eastern shore of the Mediterranean.

At the time the big cargo vessel was built to convey the obelisks from Karnak up the Nile the Phoenicians themselves were laying plans for building a new kind of sailing ship, one that would carry them to the western limits of the great inland sea and even beyond. Princess Hatshepsut, who has been termed ' the first great lady in world history,' sent her own ships on an expedition to the land of Punt, beyond the Red Sea, presumably to bring back gold and incense and spices, especially incense, which was worth considerably more than its weight in gold, for the priests of Ancient Egypt consumed vast quantities of it in their temples and in the embalming of the mummies that peopled the temple vaults. However, the ships of Hatshepsut were not as seaworthy as the vessels of the Phoenicians, and so the Egyptians were encouraged to trade with their neighbours in Phoenicia, who began to make the Mediterranean their own domain for trade. Five hundred years after history's first great lady was murdered the Phoenicians, under orders from their King Hiram of Tyre,

13

manned some of Solomon's ships in Eziongeber, the Akaba that
Lawrence of Arabia captured, and sailed with the Israelites for the
legendary Ophir, from which, according to the Bible, they
brought back ' gold, and silver, ivory, and apes, and peacocks'.

By this time the Phoenicians had colonized such Mediterranean islands as Malta, Sicily, and Sardinia and founded in
south-west Spain a port they called Gades, but which Francis
Drake knew as Cadiz when he entered its harbour to singe the
beard of King Philip. They had also founded a city on the north
coast of Africa, which they named Tingis and we today know
as Tangier. Trade developed the commercial sinews of the maritime Phoenicians. They grew rich and ever more enterprising.
Somewhere around 800 BC they founded a fresh North African
colony, which they named Carthage. It provided a springboard
port from which the more daring Phoenician sea-captains set
off on voyages through the Pillars of Hercules, as they called the
Straits of Gibraltar, southward along the African coast and northward to the Tin Islands, as they referred to Britain. In their
single-sailed ships they carried the trade goods of their day,
wares wrought in bronze and other metals, ornaments and
pottery, and bales of the famous purple cloth of Tyre. In exchange for these they accepted tin and other raw materials
from Britons working the ancient mines of Cornwall, while from
Madeira and the Canaries they brought back to the Mediterranean the raw vegetable dyes to be used by the craftsmen in
Tyre and Sidon.

However, time wrought changes of a kind that are familiar
today. The colonists of Carthage grew strong enough to claim
their independence and then to challenge the mother country. A
little more than three hundred years after the founding of Carthage the Carthaginians sailed across the Mediterranean and
occupied southern Spain. A new naval and military power had
been established on the shores of the inland sea. Within five
years Carthaginians under Hamilco had arrived off the shores
of Britain, and the tin miners of Cornwall had new customers
for their ore.

About the same time another Carthaginian leader, named
Hanno, who was a relative of Hamilco, collected an even larger
fleet and prepared to sail after him through the Pillars of Hercules, and then head south, instead of north.

Hanno was a true explorer. He sailed to make discoveries and to find new lands, and because he was a wise man he went well prepared, accompanied by sixty vessels, each of which was manned by fifty rowers to overcome squalls and calms alike. These ships carried three thousand men and women who were to become Hanno's new colonists, and with them went the stores and supplies necessary for starting a colony.

As a matter of fact, Hanno founded not only one colony, but six, and each was named by him. The sixth was a settlement on Cape Juby in the latitude of the Canaries. But having landed his colonists and their stores and equipment, Hanno did not turn his ships around and head north for the Pillars of Hercules and home.

He continued to sail south.

It can be expected that some of his captains and undoubtedly many sailors among his crews found in this insistence on sailing into the unknown a cause for complaint. But if his men's grumbling reached his ears Hanno remained unmoved by the fears they expressed.

For Hanno was, like a good many great explorers who followed him, a man led by a dream.

The dream was to emulate other explorers whose stories had come down the ages out of the mists of history. First, there was the story of Pharaoh Necho. He had, in effect, led a private expedition in a circumnavigation of Africa, but taking the opposite course from that followed by Hanno. Second, there was the legend of mariners in the time of Princess Hatshepsut having sailed around Africa, and some said Necho had traced the course of those early Mediterranean mariners whose great feat was lost in the mists of time.

Just how much was accomplished by those early explorers who faced incredible hazards in craft never designed to withstand the seas they had to encounter is largely speculation plus a tongue-in-the-cheek record by the Greek writer Herodotus, who was certainly impressed by Necho's voyage sufficiently to put it on record for all time.

To Herodotus Africa was Libya. He wrote :

' The shape of Libya shows that, save for the part that borders on Asia, it is surrounded on all sides by sea. The first to bring

15

proof of this, as far as I know, was Pharaoh Necho of Egypt. When he ceased digging the canal which was to link the Nile and the Red Sea he equipped an expedition and commanded it to sail round Libya through the Pillars of Hercules, back into the Mediterranean, and so return to Egypt. Therefore the Phoenicians left port and sailed out of the Indian Ocean into the southern sea.'

Like Solomon bound for the riches of Ophir, Pharaoh Necho took Phoenicians with him, for he was obviously impressed by their maritime skills and know-how with ships and the finer points of sailing and navigating them. Hanno, who came of Phoenician stock originally, quite probably felt himself continuing a tradition by leading his colonists and explorers into the Atlantic and trying to circumnavigate Africa in the reverse direction from Necho. He was certainly emulating them by taking colonists, for as Herodotus continues:

' When autumn fell they landed, tilled the fields, and waited for the harvest in whatever part of Libya they happened to be. When they had harvested the corn they sailed on, until after two years they sailed through the Pillars of Hercules, and so returned to Egypt again in the third year. They related, which I cannot myself believe, though perhaps some other may, that as they rounded Libya they beheld the sun on their right hand.'

In short, which Herodotus found hard to believe, the sun was shining to the north of the expedition, instead of to the south. Yet this is precisely where it would shine had Necho's ships journeyed across the equator from north to south, as they must to round Africa.

So the very claim Herodotus could not accept as true would appear to vouch for the genuineness of the old-time mariners' story!

Hanno did not equal the feat of Pharaoh Necho simply because he was trying to establish permanent settlements. To do this he had to leave stores he could have used for continuing his voyage. He was also putting his experiences on record, the first exploring navigator to do this. The narrative was taken down by a scribe and later chiselled into a tablet that was

When stones came flying to meet the Carthaginians they caught them
on their shields and continued to advance

STORIES OF FAMOUS EXPLORERS

placed in one of the temples in Carthage. The tablet disappeared at the time of the sack of Carthage, but by then a Greek translation had been made. This is known as the *periplus* of Hanno.

The narrative relates how the explorer reached what he called the Chariot of the Gods, today accepted as Mount Cameroon, which is not far from the equator. This was where he had reluctantly to listen to the grumblings of his men, for provisions were very low, and give the order to turn about and sail north again.

In the *periplus* Hanno relates:

' We had now been sailing for four days and throughout each night we saw the land full of flames; in the midst of them was a very tall flame that towered above the other flames and seemed to reach up to the stars. By day we saw that it was a very high mountain. We named it the Chariot of the Gods. When we had sailed along beside streams of fire for three days we came to a gulf called the Southern Horn. In the depths of this bay lay an island. Upon it was a lake, and in the lake an island peopled by crowds of savages. Most of them were women with rough, hairy bodies.'

Hanno had with him some natives he had taken aboard at a previous point of call. One of them told him the hairy savages were called gorillas. Having been forced back to his ship when he tried to land off the mouth of a river that must have been the Senegal, Hanno now decided not to be turned back again by a shower of stones.

He gave the order to land, and this time when stones came flying to meet the Carthaginians they caught them on their shields and continued to advance until they were splashing out of the sea and across a sandy shore.

The *periplus* records:

' We pursued them. We could not catch the males; they escaped by flight. They were able to leap away over the rocks and kept us at bay with stones. Three of the females, who absolutely refused to follow, defended themselves against our men so violently by biting and scratching when we captured them that we killed them. We then flayed them and brought back

18

their skins with us to Carthage. As we had come to an end of our provisions, we did not continue our journey any farther.'

It seemed likely that these agile creatures were chimpanzees, rather than actual gorillas. Their descendants did not see a white face until some two thousand years later, when Prince Henry the Navigator came round the bulge of Africa, another explorer following a dream.

Indeed, when Hanno turned for home he may have experienced some disappointment, but he was a man with a story to tell. Following the indentations of the African coastline, he had covered considerably more than six thousand sea miles. He had founded settlements, and he had his preserved skins of man-like creatures which were to provide the origin of another legend, that of ' the wild men of the woods ', believed in up to the days of Linnaeus, the famous Swedish botanist of the eighteenth century.

We know nothing of Hanno's adventures on his return voyage to Carthage, and only one conclusion can be drawn from the way his narrative on the temple tablet was received. His fellow Carthaginians were not encouraged to pay the expense of further such expeditions down the African coast. So as a great explorer Hanno takes his rightful place in history, but as an empire-builder his name is forgotten, like that of the unknown Carthaginian sea-captain who arrived at the Azores with a supply of coins, which he dumped in an earthenware vessel and left behind when he hoisted sail and headed back to the Pillars of Hercules.

This discovery of the Azores by the Carthaginians is another half-fact, half-legend piece of lost history. The pot holding the coins was discovered somewhere in the middle of the eighteenth century. A great storm at sea had resulted in a severe pounding of the shore of the island of Corvo, which is not far from the other island of Flores, off which Sir Richard Gren-ville in the *Revenge* fought a memorable sea battle in 1591. When the storm had abated and the abnormal tide receded it was found that some ancient ruins on the beach had been shifted. Uncovered was the earthenware pot, black from long-dead fires, and containing coins struck in Carthage and

Cyrenaica in the early years of the fourth century BC.

These coins exist in no modern museum because they have been lost. Their finding was recorded, the coins themselves were carefully described, and experts are satisfied that the story is true.

So accordingly must be its implications. Someone who possessed the coins when they held currency arrived on the island of Corvo to the north-west of the Azores. No suggestion that they had been washed up on the island is tenable because the ocean currents flow from the island, not towards it. So the coins were brought ashore by someone who arrived on a vessel from Europe. The vessel, of course, might have been driven before the lashings of such a storm that uncovered the fire-blackened pot in the eighteenth century. The owner of the coins might not have returned to his homeland. But somehow he arrived nearly a thousand miles out in the Atlantic with a nearly complete set of Carthaginian coins covering the years 330 to 320 BC.

Whatever the true story of the coins in the earthenware pot, it is a matter of history that, following upon the return of Hanno from his explorations along the west coast of Africa, merchants in Europe, who had the major interest in the opening up of new lands and fresh sea-routes to those already known, turned to the east.

Out of the east had arrived the nomad tribes in the dawn of history to settle on the Mediterranean shores. They had been followed by such conquerors as Darius and Alexander, who brought with them the overtones of oriental civilizations and fresh legends of far lands and fabulous cities. Names that brightened the eyes of European merchants were those of Persia and Arabia, India and distant Cathay. Expeditions were paid for whose object was to find routes to these eastern lands so that trade could flourish. Some went overland, others left the Red Sea to face such unknowns as the unrelenting monsoons, which are reputed to have been recorded by an unnamed Roman collector of taxes.

According to the story he was in a ship that was blown directly across the broad expanse of the Indian Ocean from the mouth of the Persian Gulf. After a terrifying journey his vessel arrived off Ceylon.

When he ventured ashore and related his experiences he was

gravely informed that if he had patience he could surely return whence he came. When he pressed for further information he was told what must have seemed a very tall story indeed. He had only to wait for some weeks, and the wind that had brought him would be blowing in the opposite direction.

The story relates that he waited because there was nothing else he could do. Upon the wind changing direction he set out again for the Persian Gulf, and was amazed to discover that what he had been told was no less than the truth. He was blown back the way he had come by a returning wind.

He arrived eventually on the shores of the Mediterranean and told his experiences. To the merchants and European sea-captains it was almost as though they had received a divine sign of the direction in which to send their caravans and sailing vessels.

Trade with the east gathered momentum with the rise of Rome and the decline of Carthage during the Punic Wars. Roman generals with their armies criss-crossed Europe and spanned the lands of the Near East. Spices and aromatics found their way westward, for in the wake of the armies travelled the merchants.

The process went on for hundreds of years, with Europe's trade facing east and merchants beginning to deal with Arabs who, when the north-east monsoon was blowing, brought valuable cargoes along the Malabar coast and across to the ports set up along the Gulf of Aden.

Stories began to be told of the land of the Great Khan to the east, of fabulous cities like Calicut and Canton. Traders became explorers. The caravan routes of ancient times were followed, and dhows and galleys crossed the sea lanes east of Africa.

But Africa along the western coast remained unexplored. The Atlantic beyond the Pillars of Hercules of classical days was a vast sea waste, uncharted, unchallenged by the sea-captains of the maritime states that rose to power in the Mediterranean lands with the eventual fall of Rome and the spread of Christianity.

The galleys of some of these states dominated the narrow seas, holding the trade lanes for the new breed of merchants against encroachment by the navies of other states. Ironically some of the ancient knowledge was lost or forgotten. For instance, although Herodotus seems clearly to have understood that the African continent was a vast island, Ptolemy, the most famous of antiquity's geographers, astronomers, and map-makers, believed that the Indian Ocean was really an inland sea, like the Mediterranean. Its southern shore was the coastline of Africa, running eastwards to Cathay.

Ptolemy flourished around AD 150, half a century after those Carthaginian coins found in the Azores were minted and some seven hundred years after Pharaoh Necho had circumnavigated the continent.

What Necho had discovered became lost knowledge to mariners who believed the fanciful maps of Ptolemy to be accurate. For thirteen hundred years those maps were trusted, until the Portuguese reached the Cape of Good Hope, late in the fifteenth century.

But by that time a new age of exploration was beginning. Before it could begin other intrepid explorers and wanderers across the known world into unknown regions were to make their journeys and return with knowledge that was to help change men's views about the world in which they lived.

Surprisingly one of the greatest feats of exploration was made by Northmen living far from the warm lands of the Mediterranean, men who lived frugally by Mediterranean standards, but whose courage and determination were of a kind to match those of Pharaoh Necho and the Carthaginian Hanno. They too were men who appeared out of the mists of time.

For just as Hanno was two thousand years ahead of the Portuguese who followed him, so Leif the Lucky was at least five hundred years ahead of Colombus in reaching the American land mass.

THE VIKINGS OF VINLAND

KING Alfred the Saxon, whom men were to call the Great, leaned back in the big oaken chair that served as his throne in Winchester. He stroked his long flaxen moustache as his blue eyes shrewdly assessed the man standing before him. Othere the Norse sea-captain was a big man with a booming voice and a chin that tilted aggressively. He had been invited by Alfred to teach the king's seamen how he and his mariners handled their ship, for Othere was a voyager of great experience, whose home was in Halogaland, in the north of present-day Norway, and he had completed a notable sea journey to the White Sea and sailed up the river known today as the Dvina.

'Tell me of your homeland,' Alfred invited the man before him.

'The country of the Northmen,' Othere told him, 'is exceeding long and narrow. Because it is mountainous little can be pastured or ploughed, and that only by the sea, and even there bare rock is for ever cropping up. Eastward are wild waste mountains where Finns dwell. Sometimes we make war on them.'

'Where is your home, Othere?' Alfred asked.

'I live in the north,' the king was told, 'in the land by the west sea, and no man dwells north of me, though the land stretches far, for all is waste, save that here and there a few Finns come for hunting in winter and in summer for fishing in the sea. It was to find out how far the land ran north, and whether any man dwelt there, that I made my voyage.'

23

Othere's voyage to the White Sea was made some time about the year 870.

Another sea-captain who entered Alfred's employ was Wulfstan, who explored the unknown regions of the Baltic Sea and reached Estonia and the Vistula. Wulfstan's voyage was made about the same time as Othere's and it is remarkable that both explorers set out on their expeditions from the same port.

Both voyages are also remarkable for two other reasons. First, they were placed on record by a royal hand. Second, the men who made them sailed eastwards to explore. Hitherto the Northmen and Vikings had sailed west. They had founded colonies in both Britain and Iceland, which was in the same latitude as Othere's homeland of Halogaland, and had sunk roots. Family ties among the Vikings were strong, and the members of a family who settled elsewhere made journeys, often of considerable length, to visit the others.

So that it was not a strange thing for young Bjarni Herjulfson to sail from his father's home at Eyar, in Iceland, to visit friends and relatives in Norway just about a hundred years after Othere stood in Alfred's big hall in Winchester and told of his voyage round the North Cape to the White Sea and the region where today stands the Soviet city of Archangel. Bjarni Herjulfson sailed back to Iceland in the summer of 985, but he found a surprise awaiting him. His father's home was deserted.

'He has sailed to join Eric the Red,' neighbours at Eyrar told him. 'What will you do now?'

'I'll sail to join him,' said the young man.

Eric the Red had settled in Greenland. If Bjarni was to be sure of reaching Greenland in time to spend the winter with his father he knew he had best lose no time in again hoisting the sail of his longship with the dragon head at its prow. He took aboard provisions, held counsel with his crew, and when he raised his hand the sail was unfurled and Bjarni Herjulfson felt the timber beneath his feet rise and fall as his ship headed for the open sea to the west of Iceland.

It was to be a voyage that made history.

He held to a westerly course for three days, when the mountains of Iceland fell below the horizon behind him, more than a hundred miles away. He was then about eighty miles from Greenland, when suddenly a mist came down and a wind blew out of the north. The Viking longship had no alternative but to run before the weather coming out of the north. However, allowing for the East Greenland Drift, it is reasonable to suppose that Bjarni's general direction was in a south-westerly direction. This state of the weather continued for some days before the wind ceased, the fog-like mist cleared, and the chilled mariners were again warmed and cheered by the sun. But neither young Bjarni nor any of his crew had any notion of where they were in that waste of sun-burnished sea. Bjarni had not previously sailed to Greenland. He decided that if he continued westward he must reach the Greenland coast in due course.

He continued westward for a full day, when suddenly the lookout shouted that there was land ahead.

This must be Greenland at last, Bjarni decided. He held on the westward course until he and all his men could plainly see the trees on the hills of the land ahead. He had missed Greenland and was off what today is believed to be the region of Hamilton Inlet in the south of Labrador. In short, the Viking longship of Bjarni Herjulfson had arrived off the mainland of North America.

Knowing he had come too far south, the young Viking turned his ship north, keeping within sight of the coast and after two days sighted forests. The crew wanted to land and procure wood and fresh water, but for some reason Bjarni distrusted the dark forests. He insisted on sailing on, with a south-west wind filling his sail. He came in due course within sight of fresh land, and saw mountains and sun gleaming on glaciers, but he was looking for Greenland's pastures, of which he had been told, and could not see them.

' This is not Greenland,' he told his amazed crew.

He was right. He was standing off the south of the land known today as Baffin Island. Seeing that his men looked bewildered, Bjarni stood out to sea again. The south-west wind became a gale, which the longship rode out under furled sail for four days, at the end of which time they saw land ahead which really was Greenland.

Bjarni Herjulfson had gone the long way round to find his father, but he had discovered the New World *en route*. He settled in Greenland and gave an account of his remarkable voyage in which he sighted three different lands.

The Viking most interested in Bjarni's narrative was the son of that Eric the Red who had been joined by Bjarni's father Herjulf. Eric himself was a wild, tempestuous man who had been born in Stavanger, in Norway, but had gone to Iceland with his colonist father Thorvald Asvaldson. However, too many violent quarrels resulted in his being banished, and Eric had landed in Greenland, where he became chief of the Vikings who followed him.

Eric's son was named Leif, and Bjarni's story excited his imagination and left him with a growing feeling of wanderlust. There is an ancient Norse record called the *Heimskringla*, otherwise *Lives of the Norse Kings*, which was penned in Iceland around the end of the twelfth century. A passage in it relates how Leif came to arrange an expedition to return to the land Bjarni had found.

It was about the year 1000 when Leif and his Vikings sailed from Greenland, their shields hung along the gunwhales of their ship, and headed in the general direction taken by Bjarni Herjulfson fifteen years before. Steering south-west, Leif brought his ship to the coast of Labrador, which he named Helluland, the country of flat stones. He thought little of this new land and kept to a southerly course which brought him to what is now Nova Scotia and an island covered with tall grass and trees which in all probability was Prince Edward Island. This more inviting coastline he named Markland, the country of the woods. By this time Leif was keen to explore farther, so after clearing Nova Scotia he headed westward until he came to the region of Cape Cod, where he found wild grapes in abundance and named the country Vinland.

Winter was upon these sturdy Vikings who had reached a new continent, so they beached their longship and prepared to spend the winter months ashore. They built a fine settlement of stout houses from the ample timber supply the land afforded, but instead of the harsh bitter winter of Greenland they found the days very much milder, with the sun often warm enough to make them perspire as they worked. When the days began to lengthen again they loaded their ships with as much of this fine Vinland timber as they could stow, and then started for Greenland.

At first the Skrellings were friendly and showed their willingness
to trade

With their story told, the Greenland Vikings decided Leif had been lucky indeed to find Vinland, and men began to call Leif Ericson by a new name – Leif the Lucky. Other expeditions were fitted out to reach this land of Vinland the Good, as Leif is said to have described the country in the ancient sagas. The Vikings were primarily interested in obtaining good timber for new boats and for houses. On one of these expeditions sailed Thorvald Ericson, the younger brother of Leif the Lucky. But the Greenland Viking most entranced by the stories of Vinland the Good was Thorfinn Karlsefni. He planned to take an expedition to Vinland that would establish a Viking colony, and he worked hard to make this possible.

It was in the year 1003 that the Karlsefni expedition at last got under way and sailed towards the setting sun. According to the sagas, the ambitious Karlsefni had talked some hundred and sixty men and five women into accompanying him to Vinland. They even took aboard their ships a number of cattle, encouraged by Leif the Lucky's story of the high quality of the pasture to be found, and from this fact it can be assumed that a number of the would-be colonists were farmers, anxious to grow fat in a land where the sun was warm in winter and grapes grew wild.

Just how many ships Karlsefni had to transport his colonists and their equipment is not told in the sagas, nor is there any reference to how long the voyage took. But it is known that he eventually arrived in Vinland. It was springtime and throughout the long days of summer the colonists worked long and industriously and the colony thrived, though not without a few shocks.

One of these was the discovery that they did not have the land to themselves. In fact, it was already settled, by natives with a coppery skin who wore feathers in their hair and carried small-headed hatchets in their bead-ornamented belts. The Vikings gave these natives a name. They called them Skrellings or Skraelings. A later age was to know them as Red Indians.

At first the Skrellings were friendly and showed a willingness to trade. They bartered furs for milk and cheese made by the Viking women. They also showed a keen interest in the battle-axes and heavy swords and shields of the Vikings. The Skrellings were allowed to come and go about the colony as they pleased.

By the end of that first winter in Vinland the small colony had increased. Gudrid, Thorfinn Karlsefni's wife, had presented the leader of the expedition with a new son.

He was named Snorri, and was the first white child to be born in the New World.

When the days were again drawing out and the first leaves were colouring the trees Karlsefni's colonists were ready to embark and return to Greenland.

They had lived in the New World for two years, and when they finally stepped into their ships and hoisted sail they were settlers retreating from history, which they had certainly made.

However, so complete was their withdrawal that they left behind no lasting memorial of their occupancy of a strip of New England coastline.

Their return to Greenland did not mean the end of voyages by Viking ships to the American mainland, for the sagas tell of other sailings in search of timber and furs which were made at varying intervals over the next few hundred years, until the last Viking ship sailed from Greenland westward in the year 1357.

For some three hundred years the stories of the exploratory exploits of Bjarni Herjulfson and Leif Ericson were told as living folklore until the famous sagas and eddas were penned, relating the prowess of heroic members of various Viking families. Then the stories were narrated in lasting form for all time. Indeed the story of Thorfinn Karlsefni and his two-year settlement on the coast of Massachusetts is related in the narrative that is entitled by the writer *The Saga of Eric the Red*. Because of the historical importance of the settlement the narrative has come to be known equally well as *The Karlsefni Saga*.

Today there is a splendid monument in the city of Boston to Leif the Lucky, the first white man to step ashore in the New World and perceive its possibilities for the future. But Leif Ericson has still another claim to fame. He was the leader who introduced Christianity into Greenland. Eric the Red, his father, died a pagan, believing, though perhaps not too devoutly, in the old Norse gods of his Viking forebears. It is certain that when men named Eric's son Leif the Lucky they felt the God of the Christians had protected him on his voyage to discover the lands of Vinland and Markland. Yet by the time Columbus reached the New World the Viking colony in Greenland was fading into obscurity.

That was five hundred years after Leif Ericson had waded ashore and picked the wild grapes of Vinland.

Throughout the greater part of that half-millenium the westward voyaging of the Greenland Vikings continued sporadically, as the following reference in the *Icelandic Annals* of the Bishop of Skalholt for the year 1347 proves:

'There came a ship from Greenland, even smaller than the little Iceland-farers. It sailed into the outer Straumfiord and had no anchor. It bore seventeen men who had sailed to Markland.'

Seventeen men, that is, who had sailed to the New World in search of good timber to be brought back to Greenland. Just about two hundred years later, in 1541, a Hanseatic ship from Hamburg, the *Kraffel*, captained by Gert Mestemaker, arrived off Greenland. The object of the voyage was to develop fresh trade for the members of the Hanseatic League. But although Mestemaker went ashore he found no one with whom he could open negotiations. He returned to Hamburg.

The Vikings had vanished into history.

THE GENOESE PRISONER

O N A bright September day just fifty years before the Black
Prince won his spurs at Crécy a cabin boy tumbled down the
steps of a Venetian galley in the Adriatic. Before he reached the
captain's cabin he was shouting with excitement.

' Signor Polo! Signor Polo! The Genoese fleet is in sight.'

The door of the captain's cabin opened. Out stepped a man
about forty, with bronzed lean face and quick darting black eyes
under his long dark hair.

' I'm coming, boy,' he called. ' I'm coming.'

He sounded a little tired. Or perhaps his lack of enthusiasm
for the promised sea-fight was more due to the fact that he was
not a sea-captain by choice. His family was rich, and now war
had started with Genoa the wealthy families of Venice had been
ordered by the Doge and his council to provide galleys and arm
them for the new struggle against the rising power of the
Genoese.

Captain Polo reached the deck as signals were sent from the
galley of Andrea Dandolo, the Venetian admiral. Dandolo was
one of the most powerful nobles of the Venetian State. A little
more than ninety years before one of his family had been the
Doge who had diverted the Fourth Crusade to the capture of
Constantinople in 1204. As a result of Enrico Dandolo's states-
manship and shrewd diplomacy Venice had taken possession of
islands in the Aegean and parts of the eastern Adriatic mainland, as well as Crete and Salonica.

Throughout almost a century Venice had been the major
naval power in the Mediterranean, dominating trade and trade

routes and extending her influence beyond the Near East. In fact, the Polo family had done more than any other to explore the possibilities of trade all the way to the land of the Great Khan and the glittering realm of Cathay. Now the family's wealth had brought the youngest of a trio of much travelled Polos to stand on the deck of a Venetian galley and fight off the Genoese challenge.

The man of forty-two, who had travelled possibly farther than any other European save his father and his uncle, looked at the bunting on the admiral's flagship and his thoughts were mixed. It seemed a curious distance to travel to end up on a galley off the Dalmatian coast. By turning his eyes he could see the rooftops of Curzola with the sun winking on them. Then he heard a noise like distant thunder and puffs of wind beat at the sails over his head and he saw the gleam of pikes on the Dandolo galley and the big flag with the Lion of St. Mark lifting and unfurling as the stiffening breeze caught it.

The date was 7 September 1296.

Captain Polo had no great idea of his capacity as a naval commander as he stood on the deck of his galley watching the ships of Genoa bear down. Before the sun set on the Adriatic that memorable day he was cruelly confirmed in his belief. Not only were the ships of Venice defeated by those of Genoa, but Captain Polo found himself a captive.

He was ignominiously taken to Genoa and imprisoned. When his family heard of his misfortune they tried through various channels to arrange payment of a ransom for him. However, the Genoese were in no hurry to lose a prisoner who had the reputation of being a much-travelled merchant of considerable wealth. They even gave their prisoner some advice, little thinking it would be taken.

' If time hangs heavily on your hands, Marco Polo,' they said somewhat derisively, ' try writing of your travels.'

The prisoner discussed the possibility with another inmate of the Genoese prison.

' Rustician,' he asked, ' you are a scribe. Would you help me?'

Rustician is said to have come from Pisa. He too longed for an occupation that would help to shorten days that seemed endless.

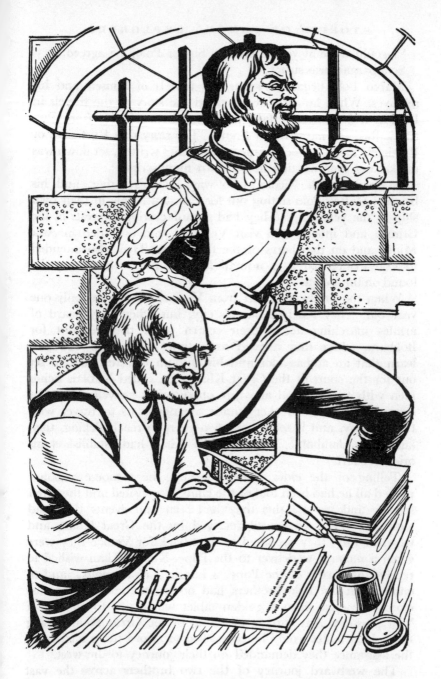

Marco Polo began to relate the travels of himself and his relatives

' I could write at your dictation, Signor Polo,' he agreed.

So a bargain was struck.

Marco Polo began to relate the travels of himself and his relatives. While he certainly dictated the story of the travels in Italian, it is almost certain that his fellow-prisoner from Pisa transcribed the narrative in French. The story that Rustician, or Rustigielo as the scribe's name is sometimes written, set down was unlike any then existing in a known manuscript.

It opened with Nicolo, who was Marco's father, and his brother Maffeo Polo setting out for Constantinople in their own ship in the year 1255. They had manufacturing interests in the Crimea and intended to visit Venetian traders settled in Asia Minor and on the shores of the Black Sea. They also intended to visit Prince Barca, a nomad Mongol ruler who was to be found on the Volga.

When the brothers set out from Venice, Marco was only one year old. They reached Barca's city, but when they heard of armies marching across their return route they set out for Bokhara, where they arrived some time in the year 1260, to learn that an ambassador and his entourage were about to set out for the court of the Great Khan men called Kublai. Being men with a vision and also rare opportunists as well as men of courage, the Polo brothers made arrangements to travel with the embassy, and it took them two years to reach Peking, then known as Cambaluc, where Kublai Khan had established his oriental court.

Telling of the elder Polo's journey, the Genoese prisoner related all he had been told of the lands they visited and the often strange and novel sights they had seen and events they had witnessed. They were well received by the Great Khan, and when in 1265 they prepared to start back for Venice they were given a message to deliver to the Pope. Kublai Khan wished to receive, as envoys of the Pope, a hundred pious monks, and to ensure that the Polo brothers had no trouble crossing his vast empire he gave them a golden tablet which was to serve as a VIP passport. Any subject or vassal of the Great Khan seeing the golden tablet would be compelled to afford the travellers all the assistance they demanded on their journey to the west.

The westward journey of the two brothers across the vast expanse of trackless Asia took three years. When at last they

arrived at Acre it was to learn that the Pope had died and
Christendom was awaiting the election of his successor. Nicolo
and Maffeo, laden with the treasures they had brought from
Cathay and the Great Khan's court, decided they had best
make straight for Venice. They arrived home at last in the year
1269, having been absent some fourteen years.

Among those who greeted them was a stranger of fifteen.
This was Marco, Nicolo's son.

Marco was the most attentive listener to the traveller's tales
of his father and uncle. He asked them countless questions and
seemed never tired of hearing further details of the places they
had visited and the people and princes with whom they had
stayed.

Two years later Nicolo and Maffeo were still in Venice
kicking their soft-leather heels, and the new Pope had still to be
elected by the College of Cardinals. They decided to set out again
for Cathay and report in person to the Great Khan why his
message had not been delivered.

By this time Marco was a strapping lad of seventeen.

'Take me with you,' he begged his father and uncle. 'I will
be able to make the journey to Cathay.'

Indeed, it was no journey to be undertaken lightly, and the
Polo brothers argued the matter at great length before they
found themselves agreeing to take Marco with them. Preparations for the great journey were made, and at last, in 1271, a
fresh Polo expedition set out for Cathay. Young Marco Polo
turned his back on his native Venice for what was to prove a good
many years.

The Polos arrived in due course in Acre, where the brothers
shrewdly took the precaution of obtaining a letter from a papal
legate explaining the Pope's death and why the message of the
Great Khan had not been delivered in person by them. Kublai
Khan had also requested them to obtain for him some of the holy
oil from the lamp of the Holy Sepulchre. The papal legate obtained a flask of the oil for them, and again they started out. However, they were overtaken by a messenger who sent them hurry-
ing back to Acre. The legate whom they had met had heard,
shortly after their departure, that he had been elected the new
Pope. He gave them a personal message for the Great Khan
to replace the letter he had previously written, and he ordered

two preaching friars to accompany the Venetians. The friars were to explain Christianity to the oriental prince.

Perhaps the new Pope found the project of a hundred pious monks rather daunting!

His friars, however, were not well-chosen emissaries. They may have been excellent at delivering a sermon or a lesson, but they lacked the stout hearts that characterized the three Polos. By the time they reached Armenia in the Venetians' company the friars were too scared to go farther. They made excuses and returned to Acre. The Polos continued their eastward journey.

Had they arrived at the Great Khan's court with the friars, and had the friars converted Kublai Khan to Christianity, then the entire history of mankind might well have been changed completely.

As it was, the Polos had to traverse Asia without the Pope's representatives for company. They crossed Persia to Yarkand and Shachau, where once more they presented their golden tablet as passport, for again they were in the kingdom of the Great Khan. Word of their coming sped ahead of them. In Kan-chou they were met by a special guard of honour sent at the Emperor's personal command. They were accompanied across the north of Cathay, down the river Hwang-ho, to the city that was Kublai Khan's summer capital.

At last, in May of the year 1275, Marco Polo, now a young man nearly twenty-one, stood in the great throne room of the city of Chandu and saw the dark almond-shaped eyes above the Great Khan's long drooping black moustaches, and thrilled to the knowledge that he had arrived where few men of his race had been before. He wondered much at the robe-like dresses, the richness of ornamentation, the long oiled pigtails worn by the men and called queues.

He saw the Great Khan smile at his attempt to conceal his bewilderment. Through his interpreter Kublai Khan told Nicolo, ' If your son Marco is willing to enter my service he shall be received with honour.'

It was an invitation that could not be refused.

The young Venetian found himself installed as a private secretary to the greatest and most formidable prince of the Middle Ages, half the world away from his own home!

Marco Polo grew to full manhood in the service of Kublai

Khan, for he remained in Cathay for no less than seventeen years. When the Khan's warriors wrested the province of Manzi from the Sung Dynasty, to the south, Marco Polo was appointed its Governor and he went to live in a palace in the capital of Yang-chou.

In his Genoese prison fortress the man who had lived such incredible years thousands of miles away in what was, in truth, a different world, remembered his crossing of the vast plateau of the Pamirs.

'The region is so lofty and cold,' he told the man from Pisa who was patiently putting words to parchment, 'that you do not even see any birds flying, and I must notice also that, because of this great cold, fire does not burn brightly, nor give out so much heat as usual, nor does it cook food so effectively.'

Possibly the Genoese prisoner was reminded of the difficulties of cooking food by a slender prison diet. But he told of warmer climes and lands where the sun shone brightly, and he described in detail the mighty Emperor who ruled so many provinces of Asia.

At his dictation the man of Pisa wrote:

'I shall tell you of the great and wonderful magnificence of the Great Khan now reigning, by name Cublay Khan – Khan being a title which signifieth the Great Lord of Lords, or Emperor. And of a surety he hath good right to such a title, for all men know for a certain truth that he is the most potent man, as regards forces and lands and treasure, that existeth in the world, or ever hath existed from the time of our first Father Adam until this day.'

Closing his eyes, the middle-aged prisoner could transport himself to that far-off glittering court and see again the personage who was a fable in the west. He told the scribe:

'The personal appearance of the Great Khan, Lord of Lords, whose name is Cublay, is such as I shall now tell you. He is of a good stature, neither tall nor short, but of a middle height. He has a becoming amount of flesh, and is very shapely in all his limbs. His complexion is white and red, the eyes black and fine, the nose well formed and well set on.'

He related how the Great Khan ruled through twelve barons

who were overlords of thirty-four vast provinces, and went into great detail about the various forms of currency made from the inner bark of mulberry-trees, adding rather enviously, ' The Khan causes every year to be made such a vast quantity of this money, which costs him nothing, that it must equal in amount all the treasure in the world.'

Marco Polo's employment throughout his seventeen years in the Great Khan's service was not restricted to China. He once journeyed to Tibet as a special envoy of the Great Khan, and another time he made a difficult trip to Burma on his master's behalf, and again he went south to the China of the Sung Dynasty.

All these lands and their peoples were described by the man languishing in the prison in Genoa. His memory was truly fantastic, and it is possible that, had he not sailed the family galley against the Genoese and been taken prisoner, he would never have considered putting his experiences in some form of permanent record.

He described palaces ' entirely roofed with gold, just as our churches are roofed with lead ' and ' a kind of black stones existing in beds in the mountains, which they dig out and burn like firewood ' and recalled that ' the Emperor moreover hath taken order that all the highways travelled by his messengers and the people generally should be planted with rows of great trees a few paces apart – and thus these trees are visible a long way off, and no one can miss the way by day or night.'

Even so, he might never have reached Venice to be taken prisoner by the Genoese had not chance favoured the Polos. For after seventeen years spent in the lands of the Great Khan they desired to return to Venice with the vast wealth they had all three amassed. But Kublai Khan was most reluctant to allow them to leave his service.

If they angered their oriental master by persisting in their demand to be allowed to leave for Venice they risked their lives. When there seemed no way out of a curiously grim dilemma emissaries arrived in Cathay to escort back to Persia a girl who was to wed the Persian king. She was seventeen and described as very lovely. But it was considered unsafe for her to travel by the overland route to Persia, since Tartar armies were engaged in fighting, and the only alternative route was by sea.

The emissaries from Persia begged Kublai Khan to allow the Venetians to accompany them as they were skilled in the art of navigation.

It was an occasion when the Great Khan could not lose face, for the young girl promised as a bride to the Persian king was a relative of his by marriage. So reluctantly he agreed that the three Polos should accompany the Persians and the promised bride of their king. Ships were made ready and provided with crews, and anoth~ golden passport that would guarantee safe conduct and fresh provisions *en route* was handed to the Venetians. At last they felt a fresh breeze on their faces, one blowing from the sea. The wild wide land of Cathay dropped behind them, disappeared over the horizon. The time was early in the year 1292.

It was a sea journey to match any of the Venetian's land journeys. They were two years voyaging to Persia, and in that time the expedition is said to have lost six hundred men. When the emissaries, with the bride-to-be and the Polos, arrived at the Persian court, it was to find the king dead and his son on the throne. Fortunately for the Venetians the son of the dead king looked on the maid from Cathay and smiled. He readily supplied the Polos with an armed escort. While journeying west they heard the news of Kublai Khan's death.

By the time they reached Venice, in the year 1295, they looked very different from the well-garbed trio that had left Kublai Khan's court. Their oriental garments were in shreds, they behaved like strangers, and they had almost forgotten how to speak Italian. There is a story that their closest relatives would not accept them until they ripped apart their shabby garments and produced some of the great jewels that had been sewn into the folds.

A few months in the city on the lagoon, and then Marco took the family galley to war under Admiral Dandolo and landed in prison in Genoa.

He did not return to Venice until 1299, by which time word had spread about the story of his travels written in captivity. He married and his wife Donata bore him three daughters. Long before his death in 1324 copies of his *Travels* were being prepared in French, Italian, and Latin. But in Venice his fellow-citizens set little store by the wonderful things of which he told. Because of his constant reference to large numbers they laughed behind his back and nicknamed him Marco Milione. For instance, they decided it required a very large grain of salt to swallow his assertion that from salt manufacture in one city Kublai Khan had derived a yearly tax of six million Venetian ducats. The city was Kinsay, where, according to Marco Polo, some four to five million people lived. He called it the City of Heaven. Other Venetians were not so polite. Today we know it as Hangchow.

Only when other travellers and explorers followed in the footsteps of the Polos did Venetians and other doubting Europeans come to perceive that the story and descriptions related by Marco Polo while in a Genoese prison were indeed true. Today the *Travels* are one of the greatest books in world literature.

One of the travellers who lived to dictate his own memoirs, like Marco Polo, was a man who set out on his eastward travels in the year following the famous Venetian's death. His name was Abu Abdullah Mohammed, but he is better known as Ibn Batuta. He was a law student of good family who undertook at the age of twenty-two a pilgrimage to Mecca. But by the time he arrived he felt an urge to travel on, and he joined a caravan which took him to Russia. He continued up the Volga and past the Caspian Sea to Afghanistan and India. After a stay of several years in Delhi he journeyed on to China. Five years later he arrived back in India and set out across Persia and Egypt to the Mediterranean. When he reached Fez, in Morocco, he had been absent twenty-nine years. Nearly two years later he finished dictating his story, and the world had another volume to set beside the *Travels* of Marco Polo.

A fashion in explorer's exploits had been started which is still responsible for some of the most readable books of the present age – indeed, of every age since Marco Polo, whose original manuscript was copied out by various scribes at least a hundred times.

THE PRINCELY DREAM

S O M E thirty or forty years after the death of Marco Polo, and perhaps only two years after Ibn Batuta finished dictating his memoirs, in 1355, the earliest known version of another book of traveller's tales appeared. It was in French, although the author purported to be an Englishman, Sir John Mandeville. The first English edition was a crude adaptation of the French, and it records the travels made by the author in the Far East. Whether the travels were genuinely made is highly doubtful, and today the original author is believed to have been Jehan de Bourgogne, a professor of medicine in Liège, who stole part of his book from a guide book for German travellers to the Holy Land and part from the Asian travel narrative penned by a Friar Odoric of Pordenone. As a result, although the travels of the supposed Englishman John Mandeville were based on facts, the compiler so plagiarized and altered those facts as to make much of the book worthless as a practical guide to places and people. This was the work that gained popularity throughout Europe at the expense of Marco Polo's *Travels*.

However, the *Travels* of Sir John Mandeville and those of Marco Polo both contained a reference to the legendary Prester John. Marco Polo described him as a ruler with a land near China's Great Wall. Sir John Mandeville claimed the kingdom of Prester John was in upper India.

In the year 1428 a Portuguese prince decided they couldn't both be right. Which was a reasonably fair assumption.

He was the Infante Henrique. In English the title was Prince Henry. Actually his mother was English. He had read about

41

Prester John in the Mandeville book, and when his brother Peter returned from Venice with a copy of Marco Polo's book, and he read again of Prester John, he felt a challenge to find the legendary prince.

Since the mid-twelfth century, when Bishop Otto of Freising met the Bishop of Antioch in Syria, the story had been circulating of a Christian prince called Prester or Presbyter John whose kingdom was beyond Persia in the Orient. He was supposed to have inflicted a great loss on the enemies of Christianity at a time when the Crusaders from Europe were undergoing various defeats at the hands of the Saracens. The stories of Prester John and his invincible armies were morale boosters for the battered crusaders. Travellers who had not met him spoke of his realm and described it as a land blessed with peace and tranquillity.

Prince Henry of Portugal dreamed of finding the realm and its ruler and uniting the Christian world. For the legend of Prester John had branches. One suggested that the realm of the legendary ruler had been created by none other than John the Baptist. Another pointed to St John as its creator. The whole concept was wrapped in mystery.

Prince Henry retired to the Point of Sagres, which is one of the most south-westerly tips of the European mainland. It was isolated and washed on three sides by the grey tides of the rolling Atlantic. There he thought much about Prester John and the Arab traders and seamen who controlled the sea routes to India and China from their harbours and havens in and around the Red Sea.

He also thought about those early navigators who had written of a sea route going south down the coast of Africa. That waste of waters was known to mariners in Europe and around the Mediterranean as the Sea of Darkness. This was the sea Prince Henry decided should be explored.

He dreamed of sending caravels to the Indian Ocean and finding the land of the mythical Prester John. It was a dream that grew until it was an obsession, his very reason for living.

First he had two ships prepared and manned by the most stalwart mariners he could find.

'You are not going out to attack the Moorish shipping,' he

42

told them. ' You are going to explore the southern waters beyond
the Moroccan shore.'

To the sailors it seemed the prince had lost his wits. Where
was the profit in just sailing? What could be the purpose of such
aimless voyaging?

No answers to such questions were forthcoming from the royal
patron of a new idea of exploration. Prince Henry was too
occupied in studying such maps as he could procure and dis-
cussing his dream with navigators of known experience. He
argued with those who reminded him of the risks that Portugal
was in a favoured position to send ships into the Sea of Darkness.
She lay on the extreme western end of Europe, a veritable springboard for leaping into the unknown.

Which sounded very well. But there was a good deal of head-
shaking after the prince had left the various conferences he
called.

However, Prince Henry's ships were duly victualled, armed,
and manned, and the day came when they up-anchored and
stood out to sea. Their sails filled with Atlantic wind, and they
vanished into the unknown.

The two caravels ran into foul weather within a few days
of leaving Portugal. Battling against high seas and a raging
gale, they lost sight of each other. The quest seemed doomed
and the princely dream fated to wither.

As for the prince, he had journeyed to Lagos, where he was
striving to rouse shipwrights to enthusiasm as he urged them
to construct still more durable craft. At other times he was
consulting with master mathematicians and astronomers about
the possibility of providing tables that would depict the sun's
true position each day. For Henry realized something no man
had understood hitherto. If mariners were to sail into the unknown they must have a means of charting their position by the
sun. To him it was clear that in the future navigation was to be
every bit as important to his mariners as fresh water and
food.

But at first, when he preached this new doctrine, he found
he was talking to men who had no wish to be converted to his
views. They seemed too revolutionary. Indeed, had not Prince
Henry been a devout Christian, known for the vigour with which
he had led assaults against the Moors, and had he not been the

leader and Grand Master of the religious Order of Christ, some of his views might have earned the bitter enmity of the Church. For there were times when he seemed determined to fly in the face of Providence and the divine order of things.

The prince, however, was a dreamer to some purpose.

He felt discouraged when he was brought the news that one of his two ships had returned, and he learned of the gale that had sent his vessel scurrying back, while her consort apparently was swept onward to founder with all hands. The captain of the returned ship offered no hope that the second vessel could have survived the great gale.

' We ourselves,' he explained, ' were hove to for several days, and could not put about for home until a fair wind blew.'

The prince commended the captain for his courage and gave him money to disburse among the crew, aware that he could not prevent tongues from wagging. Hereafter men would be still more reluctant to sail his south-bound caravels.

He was brought fresh news some days later. The second ship, the one believed to have foundered, had been sighted off the coast. Henry was waiting at the quayside as a boat pulled away from the ship's side. He was the first to receive the excited captain's news.

' We have discovered a new land, my lord.'

Prince Henry no longer felt discouraged. Hearing these words, he knew he had been right to send his ships into the Sea of Darkness on a voyage of exploration. According to the ship's captain the land was an island some four hundred miles south-west into the Atlantic. It had rich soil in which many plants and trees grew, including the juniper and the dragon tree, the latter highly prized as a source of medieval medicine. Moreover, the island was seemingly uninhabited.

Henry believed his men had sighted an island that could have been seen years before by some far-ranging Genoese ships, but the Genoese had laid no claim to fresh lands in the Atlantic. It is now believed this was indeed the case. The island discovered by Henry's gale-tossed mariners was the smaller of the two main Madeira islands.

When he informed King John of Portugal of the new island, and explained that it could not be one of the Canaries, and so was not a possession of the King of Castile, he received permission to arrange for a fresh expedition to colonize the new land which was given the name of Porto Santo.

This time Henry had no trouble in finding seamen ready to sail south into the Sea of Darkness. Accordingly he planned to dispatch once more the two ships that had previously sailed under his orders. They were to be accompanied by a third ship, under the command of Bartolomeo Perestrello.

The three vessels duly arrived off the newly discovered island that was some six miles long by three wide and dropped anchor. Their precious cargoes of plants and seeds and a doe rabbit that had been kept in a cage during the voyage were unloaded. After some days spent ashore the Portuguese noted a cloud to the south of the island.

One of the three captains, named Zarco, shaded his eyes with his hands and delivered himself of the opinion, ' there will be land under that cloud.'

Some time later he proved it. He sailed his ship from Porto Santo towards the cloud, and nosed the prow into rolling surf that made the sea appear to boil. Suddenly the mists cleared and he and his men beheld ahead hills whose slopes were covered with forests through which silvery streams meandered. The surf broke on the shore of a wide inviting bay.

Zarco had discovered the cloud's secret. It was the large island today called Madeira, from the Portuguese word for ' wood '.

When news of this discovery reached the Portuguese court, Zarco was made a count. He returned to govern the southern part of the island and build a port which was named Funchal, from the Portuguese word for ' fennel ', a herb that was found to grow there in wild profusion.

Thus, after the lapse of centuries, men had left the European mainland and pushed their way south through the Atlantic to discover that new lands existed for the finding. A new age of exploration and discovery was about to dawn. Men were suddenly to realize that the sea might, as Prince Henry had dreamed, offer an alternative route to the lands of the orient.

At the Portuguese court there was cautious enthusiasm for Prince Henry's plans to send more ships into the Atlantic. The caution arose from the state of the royal exchequer.

' Your captains,' King John told his son, ' will have to make their voyages pay for themselves.'

This became a principle Henry instilled into those who sailed under his orders. Meanwhile he founded in Lagos his famous school of navigation. Instruction was provided with all the best nautical aids and instruments of the time, and its work in producing bold and intrepid navigators was to continue after its founder's death in 1460.

Not surprisingly Henry's work in founding the school and in emphasizing the importance of navigational aids for mariners trained to use them won him fame in his own time that was to continue in the years when Portugal was to challenge Spain on the seas of the expanding known world.

Men came to call him Prince Henry the Navigator. More than any other single man he was responsible for the dawning age of great exploration, and it is noteworthy that there is a direct link between the dream of Prince Henry the Navigator and the discovery of the Americas by Columbus. Perestrello, the third sea-captain to join the second expedition to reach the Madeiras, eventually was made Governor in Porto Santo. He had a daughter who found favour in the eyes of the Genoese mariner named Columbus and married him. For a time Columbus lived in Porto Santo, and there can be no doubt that he learned from his father-in-law the navigational techniques taught by Prince Henry's modern school and was stimulated by them, and by sight of the new maps Prince Henry had caused to be drawn by his school's cartographers, to have his own dream of a voyage of exploration.

Prince Henry's men discovered the Azores in 1432. Two years later southward-probing ships sailing under the prince's orders reached Cape Bojador, and a great leap down the African coastline had been made. Where the Portuguese landed they took possession.

But to get his captains and their men to sail beyond the notorious cape took great persuasion on the part of the royal navigator. The old legend of the Sea of Darkness stemming from classical times still lived in men's minds. Beyond the grim cape the sea might become so thick that a ship could be held fast in it, unable to move, or lurking sea monsters might appear to draw both ship and sailors in to the ocean's depths. Such superstitions had to be overcome, and overcoming them could be done only by cautious probing. It took seven years for Henry's most

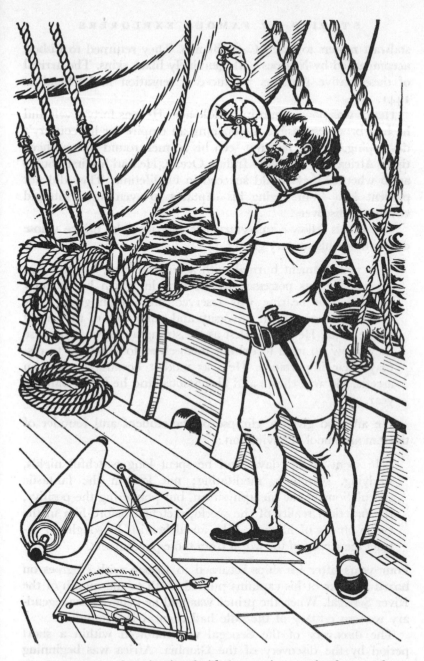

The importance of navigational aids for mariners trained to use them won him fame in his own time

stalwart miners to reach Cape Blanco. They returned to Lisbon accompanied by Negroes with genuinely black skins. The arrival of these native Africans produced a sensation in Portugal in 1441.

Henry was now a man in middle age. He was forty-seven and he had been responsible for opening an empire for his country's developing. But he had not seen his seamen round the southern tip of Africa and reach the Indian Ocean. He had his first doubts as to whether they would succeed in his lifetime. They did not prevent him from urging his captains to even more intrepid voyages of discovery.

One of his fellow-countrymen has described the prince whose dream made his country great :

' His temperament burned with a feverish heat, but this was because he was possessed by an idea in which he ardently believed. His bearing was reserved, his speech gentle. His genius was constant in adversity and quite void of the vanity of the weak. He was modest as the strong are always, because they know no need to exhibit themselves, to show off, to display their importance. He was modest because he was an ascetic. He was chaste and abstemious, and he fasted half the year.

We are also given a glimpse of the student and founder of the famous school of navigation :

' He spent all his days, and he spent long watchful nights, studying, searching, meditating; not lost in the fantastic speculations of the metaphysician, but pondering the positive, the practical reality of the world, sketched before him in the crude charts of his day. Like an alchemist, he sought to extract the secrets of the world from those parchments.'

Four years after his ships returned to Lisbon with Negroes on board another of his captains pushed south to the mouth of the River Senegal. When the prince was told he believed the legendary western estuary of the Nile had been at last found.

The discovery of the Senegal was followed within a short period by the discovery of the Gambia. Africa was beginning to yield up some of her geographical secrets.

The Genoese, who had rivalled the Venetians in the days

of the Polos more than a century before, were impressed by the news filtering out of Lisbon and Lagos, and some of their captains presented themselves before Henry and offered to sail his ships. One of them, Antonio Usodimare, took a ship to the Gambia with the novel intention of sailing up the river.

In short, while the probing of the African western coastline continued, men began to have thoughts about the interior of the continent from which the Negroes came.

Then, in 1446, a Portuguese expedition caused fresh excitement by discovering Cape Verde, where the vegetation was lush and the coastline changed direction. From running south-west, it turned south-east, and that was truly the direction in which onward-sailing sea-captains might expect to find entry to the Indian Ocean and a way to the land of Prester John.

The discovery of Cape Verde and the new direction taken by the African coastline caused Prince Henry to forget his former doubts and to entertain hope that before long the southernmost tip of Africa would be rounded by his mariners. He had sent more than fifty ships on voyages of exploration, and among his sailors were not only Genoese and Venetians, but also Germans and Danes who had heard of the new discoveries to the south of the Mediterranean.

There was trouble with Castile, who tried to claim the West African shores as an empire, and exploration was halted while Castilians and Portuguese engaged in a war that lasted through three dragging years, while Henry fretted at the delay in pushing down the African coast.

The end to hostilities came in 1455 when Pope Nicholas decided the new African discoveries were rightfully territories belonging to Portugal.

Henry lost no time in pushing ahead with a fresh expedition. In that year he commissioned Antonio Usodimare to make his famous voyage up the Gambia with one object in view. ' To reach the land of Prester John,' as the prince told the Genoese mariner.

Usodimare didn't find Prester John or his legendary kingdom. When he returned to Portugal he said he had sailed within three hundred miles of the land he sought, which was an empty boast. He said the hostility of natives who showered his ship with poisoned arrows forced him to turn about and come back. A couple of years later Henry sent another expedition in the wake of the Genoese, and these mariners reached Cantor and heard a name that was spoken by Moorish traders along the northern shore of the Mediterranean – Timbuktu.

Prince Henry was now over sixty years old and ailing. His ships had leapfrogged down the coast of Africa, opening up a new world to the astonished eyes of Europe, but the Indian Ocean had still to be reached by the sea-route.

When he died his ships had not reached the lands from which they could bring the rich cargoes of spices Europe demanded for dull diets of salted beef throughout the winter months. The Turks had captured Constantinople only seven years before the great Navigator's death, and the conquerors forbade all trade with the Christians to the west, thus halting the trade in spices between the Christian and the Arab worlds.

By the time of Prince Henry's death Europe was sorely in need of spices for medicine and to provide a healthy diet. The Portuguese kept up their leapfrogging along the African coast, even learning to sail their caravels like yachts to overcome the trade winds, and twenty-five years after the Navigator died Diego Cao reached Walvis Bay, a significant advance.

The next year, 1486, Pero de Covilhao set out with Affonso de Paiva to reach the land of Prester John by using Moorish ships in the Red Sea. They reached Aden and separated, Paiva sailing in a dhow for Abyssinia and the court of Prester John, Covilhao taking ship in another for the Malabar coast. He eventually reached Goa, destined to become a Portuguese stronghold for hundreds of years. Paiva was not heard of again.

Before Covilhao returned to Lisbon with his news Bartolomeo Dias had sailed in 1487 with two caravels and a small store vessel, which was left at Walvis Bay before a strong wind blew the caravels for almost two weeks due south, at the end of which time Dias and his suffering crews found themselves sailing due east. His men forced him to turn around for home, and in his disappointment he called the southerly point of Africa the Cape of Storms.

But the news he brought to Portugal, of the Indian Ocean being reached, caused the king to rename the southern extremity of the vast continent the Cape of Good Hope.

Dias had made the princely dream a reality. Ironically he

did not reach the east, although he had discovered the sea route to it. On another expedition to the Indian Ocean his ship foundered in bad weather off the land he had originally named – it seemed with good reason – the Cape of Storms.

BRISTOL FASHION

S E V E N years before Bartolomeo Dias hoisted sail in Portuguese waters and sailed on his memorable voyage to round the southern tip of Africa a small craft of eighty tons burden left the English port of Bristol and sailed westward.

She was the *John Jay Junior*, and she sailed out of Bristol in the middle of July 1480. She had been fitted out by merchants of the port for the purpose of reaching another legendary land.

Its name was Brazil, and it was believed to be an island somewhere to the west of Ireland.

William of Worcester, a priest who chronicled events of his time, wrote of the *John Jay Junior*:

> 'On the 18th September news reached Bristol that the ship had sailed round on the water for about nine weeks. But they had not found the island, and had returned because of heavy storms.'

The little *John Jay Junior* was not the only ship to sail from Bristol around this time. Other vessels were fitted out by the port's merchants and sent to explore the ocean beyond Ireland. But they had no success until an Italian named Giovanni Caboto arrived in Bristol with his family, settled down, and changed his name to the English form of John Cabot.

Cabot was another native of Genoa who had become a mariner when he felt the call of the sea. He was born about 1450, when Prince Henry the Navigator's fame was known in every Mediterranean seaport, but when he was eleven years old his family moved to Venice and young Giovanni became a naturalized Venetian. He grew up restless and something of a rebel, and eventually left Venice and sailed to Bristol.

What particularly attracted him to this English port is not known, but a slow fever for exploration was beginning to burn in the veins of mariners with imagination and vision, and Giovanni Caboto was certainly not lacking in these desirable qualities. Moreover, he could well have been drawn by the reputation Bristol enjoyed as a port with a firm tradition of trade, and the Italian was certainly a merchant as well as a mariner.

Indeed, a couple of hundred years after Alfred's time an eleventh-century chronicler wrote: 'The people of Bristol had an odious and inveterate custom of buying men and women in all parts of England and exporting them to Ireland for gain: nor were these men ashamed to sell into slavery their nearest relatives – nay, even their own children.' In the ensuing centuries the merchants of Bristol made changes for the better in the nature of their wares and cargoes, and at one time were the only traders permitted to send cargoes to Iceland, though it must be admitted that Bristol merchants remained historically interested in the slave trade until it was made illegal.

Another factor that may have drawn Giovanni Caboto to settle in England was Henry vii's interest in the sea and sea trading. The disruptions of the Wars of the Roses were over, a Tudor was on the English throne, and the country seemed to be enjoying a settled reign, which augured well for a merchant bent on making a profit.

The new-styled John Cabot certainly knew of Thomas Lloyd's voyage in the *John Jay Junior*, and may even have conversed with the ship's master, and with the masters of at least six other Bristol vessels that sailed on voyages of exploration after the *John Jay Junior's* return to port.

He became keen to make such a voyage himself, and when the news of the success of another native of Genoa reached England John Cabot was convinced he must emulate the daring of Columbus, who had reached the Americas in 1492. Indeed, King Henry in London was showing himself very ready to encourage any merchant with the nerve and cash to fit out an expedition to explore the western seas.

Cabot had three sons, Lewis, Sebastian, and Sancius. He talked over his ambition with them and found them ready to support him. Accordingly he made application to the king for letters patent for the discovery of new lands, and they were duly granted in 1496. The royal warrant began :

'Henry, by the grace of God King of England and France, and Lord of Ireland, to all to whom these presents shall come, Greeting.

'Be it known that we have given and granted, and by these presents do give and grant, for us and our heirs, to our well-beloved John Cabot, citizen of Venice, to Lewis, Sebastian, and Sancius, sons of the said John, and to the heirs of them, and every of them and their deputies, full and free authority, leave, and power to sail to all parts, countries, and seas of the East, of the West, and of the North, under our banners and ensigns, with five ships of what burthen or quantity soever they be, and as many mariners or men as they will have with them in the said ships, upon their own proper costs and charges, to seek out, discover, and find whatsoever isles, countries, regions, or provinces of the heathen and infidels whatsoever they be, and in what part of the world soever they be, which before this time have been unknown to all Christians.'

The full authority of the letters patent filled a long scroll, and it included the conditions that the Cabots should return from their voyage only to the port of Bristol, where whatever cargoes they brought back should be landed free of duty on the condition that a fifth of their profit from the trip should be paid to King Henry personally. Henry Tudor, it appeared, was not without some sharp trading instinct of his own.

Before leaving Venice for Bristol, John Cabot had made a journey to Mecca with the intention of discovering where precisely the Arab traders secured their spices. All he had learned was that they were procured in the distant East and were brought by various difficult stages overland to the Mediterranean. Moreover, Cabot knew of the advanced theory among learned men that the earth was of spherical shape, and not flat, so that it was possible to conceive arriving at the eastern Indies by sailing westward.

He even tried to interest the courts of Spain and Portugal

54

*So John Cabot gave his mind to dispatching stores aboard his ship
Matthew*

in this theory before finally travelling north to Bristol. Had he been listened to he might never have had to apply to Henry VII for those historic letters patent.

In the event Christopher Columbus proved more convincing to Spanish ears than his fellow-Genoese, and he sailed westward to discover the New World and call its natives Indians before Cabot received his letters patent. But it is of interest that Columbus in 1492 reached only islands in the Caribbean. He did not step ashore on the American mainland until 1 August 1498. John Cabot had trod the American mainland the previous year, 1497.

However one considers such indirect rivalry for fame, it has to be admitted that Genoa in the fifteenth century bred stout sons and intrepid mariners who were without peers in their time.

So John Cabot gave his mind to dispatching stores aboard his ship *Matthew*, moored at a Bristol quay and having a crew of eighteen, some of whom doubtless had sailed on those earlier unsuccessful voyages westward.

The *Matthew* left Bristol, but whether accompanied by another ship or not remains in some doubt. One contemporary writer claims only the *Matthew* sailed, although Sebastian Cabot later claimed two vesels left Bristol on his first expedition, but Sebastian has not been considered a trustworthy chronicler. He liked round figures and impressive claims. Unfortunately his father was only a man of action. He was not interested in writing of his experiences for posterity, and, after all, he can be forgiven for considering he was doing enough for posterity by discovering new lands to be colonized.

The *Matthew* sailed due west and undoubtedly it was John Cabot's insistence that kept the superstitious crew obeying his orders. He radiated confidence, and his men realized that when he peered at the sun he was in some mysterious way checking a predetermined course, for Cabot was one of the new-style navigators who were not intimidated by being months from their home port.

Because John Cabot was both insistent and confident, on a day early in 1497 the *Matthew* hailed within sight of land. Cabot ran forward and stared at it.

' The land of the Great Khan,' he cried excitedly.

He too thought he had reached the fabulous East of legend and mystery, the land of which Marco Polo had told so many enticing and enchanting tales. But when he stepped ashore he found himself in a barren land and the breezes that blew rather vigorously were certainly not spice-laden. His men lived on a diet of codfish because the seas teemed with them. Although it is not known where precisely he landed it is very possible that he stepped ashore on the coast of Labrador. He might even have felt cheated by a cruel fate after hearing of the reports made by Columbus on his return to Europe.

The *Matthew* left the codfish and the harsh winds and headed back to Bristol, where she arrived with no spices, no gold or treasure, and no fifth share of large profits for Henry Tudor.

No doubt he wished to encourage the men of Bristol to continue sailing westward, so Henry accepted what he doubtless considered his loss with good enough grace to donate ten pounds out of the privy purse ' to him that discovered the new isle '. It was recognition of sorts.

One person who was interested in the outcome of the *Matthew*'s westward journey was the Venetian ambassador in London. His name was Pasqualigo, and shortly after Cabot's return to Bristol he wrote to his family in Venice an account of the exploit. In his letter he said :

> ' Our Venetian who sailed from Bristol some while ago in a small vessel is back, and now relates that he reached the continent under the sovereignty of the Great Khan seven hundred Italian miles away. He sailed along three hundred miles of the coast of this land and saw no man. Nevertheless, he gave the king of that place several traps for catching wild beasts and a needle for making nets. Moreover, he found trees bearing notches. From this he concluded that the territory is not uninhabited. For reasons of prudence he re-embarked. He was away for three months. This is reliable. He lives in Bristol with his wife and sons.'

The Venetian ambassador's curious epistolary style made for seeming contradictions, but one can judge from this letter that Cabot's voyage and its outcome had made considerable impact on forward-thinking statesmen and diplomats in London. Pasqualigo was not without his Venetian pride in the fact that

57

Cabot was a citizen of Venice. 'The discoverer of this territory hoisted the English flag there,' he added in his letter home, 'but also the flag of St Mark, since he is a Venetian. So our banner has been planted in a far-off land.' He also told the family at home that Cabot had acquired the title of Grand Admiral and was treated with great honour. 'He dresses in silk,' he said a little waspishly, 'and the English run after him like fools. He, however, wants nothing to do with them.'

This last observation was not very accurate. Cabot wanted much more to do with the English, especially those living in the port of Bristol, for he was of a mind to return to the land he had discovered.

Soncino, an Italian living in London and who knew Cabot personally, had a better idea of this than the Venetian ambassador. He wrote to his master, the Duke of Milan:

'Master John has set his mind on something greater; for he expects to go farther on towards the East, from that place already occupied, ever hugging the shore, until he shall be over against an island, by him called Cipango, situated in the equinoctial region, where he thinks all the spices of the world and also all the precious stones originate.'

Cipango is the name the early chroniclers gave Japan, and this reference by one who knew Cabot is most interesting. Soncino was actually invited to go on the second Cabot expedition, to be made in the following year. He claimed that if he went and returned he would be given an archbishopric. He refused the invitation to help make history because, as he told the Duke of Milan rather slyly, 'I think the benefices which your Excellency has in store for me are a surer thing.'

In due course John Cabot received new letters patent for the fresh voyage. He was authorized to take six ships. If any of his sons accompanied him it is not known for certain. Their names are not given in the patent. But it is generally considered that Sebastian went with his father.

Again, there is little recorded information about the expedition, but it seems likely that Cabot sailed farther north, for he met icebergs in the month of July and enjoyed days with no real night. But he also sailed south, and may well have reached a very different coastline, that of Florida. Ayala, the Spanish ambassador, wrote about this voyage to his royal master and mistress, Ferdinand and Isabella. He told them :

' I think your Majesties have already heard that the King of England has equipped a fleet in order to discover certain islands and continents which he was informed some people from Bristol, who manned a few ships for this same purpose last year, had found. I have seen the map which the discoverer has made, who is another Genoese, like Columbus, and who has been in Seville and Lisbon, asking assistance for his discoveries. The people of Bristol have for the last seven years sent out every year two, three, or four caravels to search for the island of Brazil and the Seven Cities, according to the fancy of this Genoese. The king determined to send out because the year before they brought certain news that they had found land. His fleet consisted of five ships which carried provisions for one year. It is said that one of them, in which a certain Friar Buil was, has returned to Ireland in great distress, the vessel much shattered. The Genoese has continued his voyage. I have seen on a chart the direction which they took, and the distance they sailed, and I think that what they found, or what they are in search of, is what your Highnesses already possess, because it is next to that which your Majesties have acquired by the convention with Portugal.'

This convention to which Ayala referred was one based on a papal bull of Pope Alexander VI, issued in 1492, dividing the world into spheres of exploration between Spain in the west and Portugal in the east, a piece of Mediterranean diplomacy that left the English, as well as the Dutch and Germans and French, very much in the cold, where historically they had no intention of staying.

And by the time John Cabot made the second voyage to the New World he had come to consider himself an Englishman by adoption, and even a citizen of Bristol. Although little is known for certain about this voyage, and while it seems that contemporary writers managed successfully to confuse the various voyages he made, it is generally accepted today that this expedition took him to Greenland and back to Labrador, which he is reputed to have named after a certain Joao Fernandes, whom he had met in Portugal and from whom he had first heard of the western barren land. Fernandes was a *lavrador* or farmer. The story sounds far-fetched. It is also assumed by many that on the return journey Cabot rounded Cape Farewell, crossed the Davis Strait, and reached Baffin Land. Then he came southeast down past Newfoundland and Nova Scotia.

What is not in doubt is the fact that John Cabot firmly believed, like Columbus before him, that he had reached Asia. Also like Columbus, he had no conception of having discovered a vast new land mass hitherto known only to a few European wayfarers who had been more intimidated than inspired by the discovery.

He returned to Bristol an ailing man with only another couple of years of life left to him. Henry vii gave him a modest pension which was richly deserved, for not only had Bristol's adopted son with an Italian accent beaten Columbus in reaching the American mainland, but he had endured fifty-three days of rugged voyaging into the unknown to make this possible. Columbus was not at sea, on his memorable voyage in 1492, longer than thirty-three days. Moreover, the *Matthew* was a smaller craft than any of the ships making the crossing with Columbus.

Little is known of John Cabot's two sons Lewis and Sancius. Whether they ever put to sea on a voyage to the New World is very doubtful, and history might have forgotten them altogether if their names had not been included in those first letters patent of 1496.

But Sebastian Cabot was a man with a flair for self-advertisement. It is accepted that he made the first voyage with his father in 1497 and reached Cape Breton Island with him, but within a dozen years of his father's death he was in the service of Ferdinand of Spain, who employed him as a cartographer. Seven years after that he had the strange title of pilot major to Charles v.

So that one can assume he was not only much travelled, but also busy in the years immediately following his father's death. What seems almost unforgivable is that he allowed writers in the first part of the sixteenth century to afford him most of the credit that rightfully belonged to his father. It is very largely due to Sebastian Cabot's casual regard for accuracy in the matter of facts that we have today an extremely confused picture of what

60

really happened in Bristol in the years when those momentous westward voyages were being planned and prepared.

He even went to the length of giving one contemporary historian, Ramusio, a completely false account of events. The following, said to be Sebastian Cabot's own narrative, is astounding, but it is unbelievable:

' When my father died, in that time when news was brought that Don Christopher Columbus, the Genoese, had discovered the coast of India, whereof was great talk in all the court of King Henry VII, who then reigned, insomuch that all men with great admiration affirmed it to be a thing more divine than human to sail by the West into the East, where spices grow, by a way that was never known before; by which fame and report there increased in my heart a great flame of desire to attempt some notable thing. An understanding by reason of the sphere that if I should sail by way of the north-west I should by a shorter tract come into India. I thereupon caused the king to be advertised of my device, who immediately commanded two caravels to be furnished with all things appertaining to the voyage, which was, as far as I remember, in the year 1496 in the beginning of summer.'

The astounding claim continues:

' I began therefore to sail towards the north-west, not thinking to find any other land but that of Cathay, and from thence to turn towards India, but after certain days I found that the land ran towards the north, which was to me a great displeasure. Nevertheless, sailing along by the coast to see if I could find any gulf that turned, I found the land still continent to the fifty-sixth degree under our Pole. And seeing that then the coast turned towards the East, despairing to find the passage, I turned back again, and sailed down by the coast of that land towards the equinctial (ever with intent to find the said passage to India) and came to that part of the firm land which is now called Florida, when, my victuals failing, I departed from thence and returned into England, where I found great tumults among the people, and preparations for wars in Scotland; by reason whereof there was no more consideration had to this voyage.'

That last piece reads rather as though any excuse was deemed better than none for his failing to receive immediate recognition for a notable voyage.

However, what is true of Sebastian Cabot, is that in the middle of the sixteenth century he played his chair-borne part in furthering the expeditions of Chancellor and Willoughby, and so he enters another chapter of the history of exploration in his own right – eventually to die laden with more honours and pensions than his father John.

EASTWARD HO!

HISTORY had a nice sense of timing around the closing years of the fifteenth century and the early years of the sixteenth. For instance, in 1492, the year Columbus sailed for the Indies and reached the Americas, Ferdinand II captured Granada and drove the Moors from Spain. Europe was to be for the Europeans, various as they were, and so for many years were the Americas. In the year Columbus died, 1506, the foundation stone of St Peter's was laid in Rome, a symbolic end and a beginning.

That same sense of timing was just as noticeable in the intermediate years of this all-important period of exploration, not quite a decade and a half. In 1497 when John Cabot in the *Matthew* was working his way westward towards what he thought was Asia another explorer, Admiral Vasco da Gama, was sailing east and rounding the cape that had been discovered by Bartolomeo Dias. In the following year, when Columbus stepped on to the American mainland da Gama completed the searoute to India.

World events in the field of exploration were shaping with almost theatrical precision. They were certainly dramatic. Moreover, they held differences that allowed of striking comparisons.

For instance, the *Matthew* was an uncomfortable craft, paid for by her owner and master mariner. The *San Gabriel* was the largest of a flotilla of well-founded vessels paid for by the crown of Portugal, which meant by King Manoel's private purse.

She was da Gama's flagship. She was specially built for the job she undertook, and she became a convincing example to

63

the world of her day of what could be achieved by planning and know-how. Especially know-how.

For da Gama took with him a number of mariners trained in the tradition of Prince Henry's famous school. His chief navigator, Pedro d'Alemquer, was very possibly in his day the finest navigator and pilot in the world. He had done his own leapfrogging down the African coast, had crossed the ocean to Brazil, and had studied all he could learn about the Moorish ports south of the Red Sea.

As a matter of fact, da Gama took two years merely preparing to follow through after Bartolomeo Dias, and to make sure that he had the counsel of a Dias he took the famous navigator's brother Diego with him as his secretary. So far as he was able, da Gama left nothing to chance.

He was an explorer who achieved success because he deserved it by his careful and thorough preparations to make sure success was not only possible, but, given reasonable luck, even probable, having regard to the sailing conditions of the time.

The sister-ship of the *San Gabriel* was the *San Rafael,* under the command of the admiral's brother Paulo, a keen seaman with faith in the family tradition. He had for navigator another experienced mariner, John of Coimbra. A smaller caravel, the *Berrio,* named after her owner, was commanded by Nicolas Coelho, who had Pero de Escolar for his navigator, a third seaman of experience in sailing through African waters. A fourth vessel was a store-ship, which was to be considered expendable at a suitable time after rounding the Cape.

The flotilla carried some hundred and seventy mariners handpicked by the da Gama brothers, who had offered special bonuses to the men they wanted. Some ten or a dozen felons from Lisbon's jails were also carried, desperate men prepared to undertake desperate hazards in return for a fresh taste of freedom.

Vasco da Gama also took with him a number of men who knew various Arabic dialects and also Martin Alonso, who had a knowledge of some of the Bantu or Negro dialects, learned after the caravel in which he sailed on one expedition had foundered and he had spent months of forced imprisonment.

Da Gama's men, in short, were tough, hardened by a life at sea, and withal men not intimidated by danger.

64

It was Saturday, 8 July, 1497, when da Gama's flotilla weighed anchor and sailed from the mouth of the Tagus on one of the most memorable voyages in the history of exploration and discovery, and few leaving with the four ships but thought secretly that the expedition was a wild gamble and wondered what the chances were of seeing Lisbon again.

By 25 July the flotilla had arrived off the Cape Verde Islands, where the vessels took aboard supplies of fresh meat and fruit as well as stores of firewood. Their water tanks were replenished. The crews were in good heart, and so far winds had been favourable. Da Gama did not sail close to the African shore. He planned to cross the Atlantic where the area of known calms was at its narrowest point, and to achieve this d'Alemquer led the flotilla much closer to the South American continent than previous Portuguese navigators had steered. The flotilla actually crossed that papal deadline and sailed through waters which had been declared Spanish. Indeed, they sailed, by d'Alemquer's reckoning, more than eight hundred leagues from Africa, and actually saw birds that looked like heron flying south-westerly. They could not have been far from the coast of Brazil.

However, the calms delayed progress, and it was not until the first days of November that they saw the African coast again. They struck it in the general region of St Helena Bay, to the north of the Cape.

Again it proved to be, as Bartolomeo Dias had found, a region of storms. They not only were buffeted by blustery winds, but were drenched by sleet and pounded by hailstones. It was far from being a welcome to weary mariners who had been three months out of sight of land. So a short distance from the Cape the admiral gave the order for the ships to head for the shore and drop anchor. They did so under the curious gaze of natives who came to stare at these beings from another world.

One of the *San Rafael's* crew had started a diary of the expedition. He wrote in it :

' When we had gone ashore we caught one of the natives of small stature. We took him along to the ship and the commander gave him food and had him dressed in beautiful clothes, and then put him ashore again. Next day forty or fifty of them arrived, and the admiral showed them many kinds of goods to find out if similar things existed in their country – jewels, gold, cloves, cinnamon, and such like. But they understood nothing, and behaved like people who had never seen such things.'

Which was not surprising. They hadn't.

Which meant da Gama had drawn a blank at his first attempt to discover a land with treasure and spices, for those were the ' similar things ' he was eager to discover.

It was on Wednesday, 22 November 1497, that, still buffeted by high winds and pounded by strong seas, da Gama's flotilla finally rounded the important landmark of the Cape discovered by his secretary's brother. Following now closely in the wake of the dead Dias, da Gama headed for Mossel Bay, where Bartolomeo had landed. He took ashore a wooden crucifix and a stake bearing the Portuguese royal arms. A religious service was held, but many of the men could not attend it. They had been stricken by scurvy.

Indeed, scurvy became so rampant among his crews that at the end of January 1498 da Gama turned up a branch of the Zambesi and called a halt to voyaging for a month. Almost the first grisly task of the shore parties was to dig thirty graves. When later the Portuguese reached Mozambique they saw for the first time Arab dhows that had returned from India. Da Gama and his crews had now only to make the crossing of the Indian Ocean to arrive at their intended destination – the mainland of the long-sought East.

But in Mozambique, and later in Mombasa, da Gama found the aroused enmity of the Arab traders something not only to be feared, but to be avoided. In fact, had he not been lucky da Gama might have lost his life in Mombasa when the Arabs planned to attack his ships under cover of darkness. But he reached Malindi, on the Kenya coast, in safety, and soon received visitors, as the diary of the *San Rafael* seaman relates :

' Here we found four ships of Indian Christians. When the latter approached the ship of Paulo da Gama, on which the admiral happened to be, they were shown an altar-piece on which was depicted the Mother of God with Jesus Christ in

66

. . . *had him dressed in beautiful clothes, and then put him ashore again*

her arms at the foot of the Cross, together with the Apostles. And when they saw this self-same altar-piece the Indians threw themselves to the ground. During our entire stay they came in order to say their prayers and they brought cloves, pepper, and other things which they offered up.'

The promise of the long-sought spices was about to be fulfilled, and these offerings seemed an earnest of Fortune herself.

With a pilot engaged in Malindi the Portuguese set off towards the Malabar coast on 24 April. They arrived at Calicut on 20 May not to be received with open arms, but with a show of open suspicion. However, the wariness of the Calicut traders did not detract from da Gama's great achievement. He had reached India by sea. The era of Moorish mastery over the land trade routes from the Near East was over.

With the numbers of his seamen reduced, his supplies low, and his diplomacy unable to bring about much change in the attitude of the ruler of Calicut, da Gama had no recourse but to start back to Portugal. However, before he sailed on 29 August he had discovered that most of the real supplies of Oriental spices came not from India or even Ceylon, which was eight days' sail away, but from Malacca and the Moluccas or Spice Islands, much farther to the east.

In the middle of January he found himself with too few men to man his ships, and reluctantly ordered the *San Rafael* to be burned. Six months later the *San Gabriel* and the *Berrio*, encrusted with barnacles, brightwork dull and paintwork blistered, arrived in the mouth of the Tagus. Within a few weeks the price of pepper in Lisbon became a mere fraction of what it had been before da Gama sailed for the East.

Vasco da Gama himself did not reach Portugal and a hero's welcome until two months after his flagship, in September. He had remained with his dying brother Paulo in the Azores, and consequently, despite the public acclaim, his homecoming was a melancholy one. But Vasco da Gama was justly famous. In a voyage that lasted two years and two days he had taken his caravels more than twenty-four thousand miles, the distance of the earth's circumference, and he had been the first European in the new age of exploration to reach the Indies by the all-sea route.

Within a few years Lisbon had supplanted Venice as the European capital of the spice trade. Portuguese ships left Lisbon laden with spice cargoes for Falmouth, in England, and Antwerp, in the Low Countries. But some of the Portuguese captains had trouble with the rulers along the Indian coast, and in 1502 Vasco da Gama set out with fifteen ships to ensure that Portuguese trading establishments were left in peace. He was followed by Estavao da Gama in command of another five ships. A permanent Portuguese squadron was to be left in Indian waters. On this major expedition da Gama discovered the Seychelles and when his ships were attacked fought back so strongly that he crushed his attackers and took two treasure ships. Among the jewels obtained by force of arms was ' an idol of pure gold weighing sixty pounds, with eyes formed by emeralds as large as eggs, and in the chest was a ruby as big as a chestnut '.

While Spain's Conquistadores were stripping the known Americas of treasure, da Gama demonstrated that sizeable pickings were to be had in the East.

Three years later, in 1505, twenty-two heavily armed ships left the Tagus, carrying fifteen hundred soldiers, and sailed for the Indian Ocean under the command of Admiral Francisco d'Almeida. He had the title of Viceroy of India. He also had in his company a man who was to become even more famous than his commander.

This man's name was Fernao de Magalhaes, or, as it is customarily spelled in English, Ferdinand Magellan. At the time he was a young man of twenty-four who had been a page at court to the Portuguese queen. On 16 March, 1506, when the ships of the Rajah of Calicut attacked the caravels of Almeida, outnumbering them nearly twenty to one, Magellan was one of the two hundred Portuguese wounded when the sea battle was over. The navy of the Calicut ruler had been defeated, and the Portuguese were masters of the trading stations and towns along the Indian shore. The seriously wounded were sent back to Portugal, among them Magellan.

In the following year Magellan, his wounds mended, his freshly honed sword at his side, sailed on another Portuguese expedition, this time past India to Malacca, under the command of Lopez de Sequeira. If Portugal could gain Malacca she would have the largest harbour in the East Indies. At the very moment when Sequiera and his officers were toasting the success of their eastward mission they were attacked by brown-skinned Malays waving their curious but deadly sword, known as a kris. The Portuguese suffered a defeat that sent them reeling out of Malacca and heading home for Lisbon. One fighter who covered himself with glory in duelling with the kris-wielding Malays was Magellan. When he arrived in Portugal he was received as a veteran, and in 1511, when a carefully prepared expedition was launched to subdue the Malays and capture Malacca, Magellan sailed with it.

After some bitter fighting Malacca became Portuguese.

A fresh leapfrogging expedition was sent under Francisco Serrao, Magellan's good friend, to take possession of the Spice Islands. However, Magellan did not sail in one of Serrao's three heavily armed ships. He remained in Malacca, a man out of favour because on one occasion he had sided with the seamen of a ship against their officers.

He returned to Portugal, a man virtually in disgrace, in 1512. Five years later, limping with a stiff knee from a wound received in Morocco, he again returned to Portugal, asked the king for a fresh commission, and was turned down. Ferdinand Magellan's personal fortunes had reached their nadir.

On 20 October he left Portugal and crossed into Spain, where, twenty years after Columbus had sailed for the Indies, it was at last generally agreed that the rich land he had reached was not the Far East. Magellan had a bold plan to put before the Spaniards, who were enjoying their conquest of the new lands discovered by Columbus.

He had come back from sailing to the Far East in an easterly direction. He was now convinced he could do what Columbus had failed to do – namely, reach the Far East by sailing to the west.

Or, rather, to the south-west. For his bold plan was to do in a westerly direction what Vasco da Gama had done in an easterly – sail round the southern tip of the continent comprising Brazil and the lands to the south. In that way he should arrive at perhaps Cathay, and certainly the Spice Islands, which he had not been allowed to reach a few years before.

In short, Ferdinand Magellan, an intrepid soldier, a bold

mariner, sought an opportunity to reach the Far East by a door no one had so far suspected of existing.

Charles v of Spain, who had listened to Sebastian Cabot and found a post for him, now listened to Ferdinand Magellan and decided to give him authority to sail under the Spanish flag. As a matter of fact, Charles was pleased to be in a position to score off the Portuguese, as he considered it, by sponsoring the man who had been born in Oporto.

The demarcation line drawn by Pope Alexander vi had been made along a meridian 370 leagues to the west of the Cape Verde Islands, agreed in the Treaty of Tordesillas. All newly-discovered lands to the east of this line would be Portuguese, to the west Spanish. But at the time no one had pointed out that the line went through the broad shoulder of the South American continent that was marked Brazil on the charts. It is as a direct result of this arbitrary papal line that while most peoples in South America today speak Spanish, Brazilians speak Portuguese. Charles v, like Ferdinand ii before him, felt aggrieved by the loss of Brazil to the vastly growing Spanish empire. Now he perceived how he could use a Portuguese to reach the Far East to discover just where that all-important meridian continued round a world that was a sphere. It might even be that the much-talked-of Spice Islands were actually in the Spanish half of the world!

Anyway, Magellan the Portuguese was prepared, with Spanish backing, to find out.

In September 1519, two years after becoming an expatriate, he sailed in command of a flotilla of five ships for the coast of Brazil. Bad weather forced him to take shelter in a port that had been discovered by an Italian sailing under the Portuguese flag in 1501. This was Amerigo Vespucci who, on his third voyage for the Portuguese, had reached Patagonia and so established that South America was another vast continent. Indeed, it was this exploit that had resulted in his name being used to provide an alternative to the inaccurate Indies of Columbus. Mariners spoke of America as the land discovered by Amerigo Vespucci. In time this came to mean the entire New World.

Thus, in part, it was the Italian Vespucci who played a secondary role in deciding Magellan to make his famous voyage round the southern end of South America, for he had shown the similarity between South America and southern Africa.

Perhaps because he was Portuguese, and not Spanish, Magellan found himself not only distrusted by the Spaniards under his command, but actively disliked to the point where they were prepared to plot against his life. However, as an old campaigner, he had courage and could be firm. He quelled a mutiny before it could get out of hand, with his own hands clapped Vice-Admiral Cartagena, the captain of the *San Antonio,* in irons, and threatened to hang any other malcontents from his yard-arm. Strong measures, but the situation demanded them and Magellan was not afraid to provide them.

He continued his exploring way, dropped anchor in the bay of Rio de Janeiro, and went ashore to taste a new fruit, one we know as pineapple. It was eleven weeks since he had sailed from Seville. By Christmas he was heading for the mouth of the River Plate, and when he reached it and lost sight of land he thought he had already found the way to Cathay from the west. But by February he was moodily sailing south again. Then bad weather forced him to shelter in the port discovered by Vespucci, San Julian. He had to cut rations by half, announce that he would winter there, and then deal with another mutiny. His secretary, a young Italian nobleman named Antonio Pigafetta, wrote in his diary:

' For five months we stayed in the harbour, which we called the harbour of San Julian. Here much dissatisfaction and distrust rose up against Magellan. Immediately after we had dropped anchor in this harbour Magellan gave orders for dwellings to be erected on land. He also ordered the daily rations to be cut so that they would last for a longer period of time. The crews and also the captains objected to both these commands. The dissatisfied demanded to return home. Magellan refused even to discuss the matter and, when his crew persisted, he had some of the worst offenders arrested and punished.'

When he sailed on he marooned some of the mutineers and left them to their fate. Such strong action can be compared with Francis Drake's at a later date.

He had a ship wrecked in a storm, but he doggedly continued south, and one day his men were amazed to see, standing on a neighbouring cliff-top, a man who appeared at least twice as tall as a European. He wore skins and his feet, clad in fur, appeared enormous. The land was marked on Magellan's chart as Patagonia, the country of the people with large feet.

Still the southern thrust down the shore of South America continued, until on 21 October 1520, he found the strait now named after him, which was a few hundred miles long, but took Magellan a month to cover. In that month one of his ships pulled out and sailed for home the way they had come. Magellan went on to reach a placid sea which he called the Pacific Ocean. For more than three months he sailed westward, his crews subsisting on stinking drinking water, sawdust and cooked rats. Men died, many cursing Magellan, but the relentless explorer went continuously forward, thrilled by the thought that he might sail round the entire earth. He reached land in January 1521 and went on to reach the Marianas, as they are now shown on the map. Magellan called them the Ladrones, the islands of thieves, because the natives stole anything of his they could put their hands on. They even stole his skiff. On again, to reach the Philippines in April, where life ended suddenly for Ferdinand Magellan. There was a fight with some natives, and the old campaigner was killed.

His men sailed on without their captain-general and reached Borneo and eventually the Moluccas, where they loaded up with spices. But only one vessel, the *Vittoria*, was by this time seaworthy. Her captain, Sebastian del Cano, kept his men on short rations, for he feared running foul of a Portuguese flotilla in these waters. He was right, for when he reached the Cape Verde Islands and sent some of his men ashore they were promptly arrested by the Portuguese authorities.

Eighteen men completed that first voyage round the world. It had taken three years.

What had been theory was established fact.

The world was a sphere. But the men who had proved it had lost a day out of their lives, a fact which was not adjusted until diligent students realized that in circumnavigating the earth by travelling westward a solar day is absorbed. Magellan would have found the fact of interest. However, he might have been more interested to learn that, despite the tragic losses of men and ships, the *Vittoria*'s six hundredweight of spices were sold for a sum that defrayed the entire expenses of the expedition.

THE ELDORADO SEEKERS

I T W A S a few days before Christmas in 1492 when Christopher Columbus anchored in Acul Bay, off the Caribbean island of Haiti. When he returned to Spain he left men to man a fort he had built, and in his hold he carried treasure that was to prove the New World was a rich area for plundering by the conquerors who had discovered it.

When Columbus returned to the New World he journeyed as the official viceroy of Ferdinand and Isabella, his royal patrons in whose name he had taken possession of a vast empire for Spain. He had power of life and death. His royal commission proclaimed:

> ' Forasmuch as you, Christopher Columbus, are going by our command, with our vessels and our men, to discover and sub- due certain islands and continent, our will is that you shall be our admiral, viceroy, and governor in them.'

However, Columbus was a much better mariner than governor of newly acquired lands. He quarrelled with native chiefs, was recalled and replaced by men who were tyrants. They arrived and began an orgy of looting under the approving eye of the inquisition. Treasure ships heavily laden with the loot staggered from one Atlantic breeze to the next to reach Spain and pour their cargoes of gold and jewels into the large coffers waiting for them.

As an example of what this type of exploring meant to the original inhabitants of the Caribbean one can consider the changes time brought to Haiti, the island where Columbus first

stepped ashore in the New World. It has been computed that at
the time of Columbus's arrival in the *Santa Maria* the inhabitants
numbered about a million. By 1507, fifteen years later, there
were only some sixty thousand living on the island. The difference
was the death roll due to the harsh slave labour conditions im-
posed by the Spaniards under such tyrannical overlords as Don
Nicolas Ovando, who considered himself a conqueror and behaved as such.

Indeed the Spaniards called themselves the conquerors. Conquistadores is the word they used. It has passed into history with
many shades of meaning, most of them tinged with the scarlet
of freshly spilled blood.

In the early years of the sixteenth century they arrived from
Spain by the boatload, dressed in resplendent armour, with
gaudy plumes in their helmets, all prepared to go exploring
with swords in their hands and platoons of pikemen and arquebusiers at their backs. For the most part they had plenty of
animal courage as befitted the successful Christian warriors who
had driven the Moors from Spain. They considered themselves
the sixteenth-century counterpart of the medieval knights of
chivalrous reputation. They had a task to perform. Conquer
the peoples of the New World for the glory of the Spanish crown
and the glory of the God preached by the devout but grimly
uncompromising Jesuits who accompanied them.

As reward for their valour, endurance, and eventual success
under the ensign of their patron, St James, the Conquistadores
expected riches beyond their European dreams. They came to
the New World eager to find the fabulous Eldorado, the mythical
city of gold. They were strange men, upheld by faith yet blinded
by superstition, spurred on by avarice yet ruggedly willing to
endure torture when captured by vengeance-seeking natives in
the belief that they would exchange a worldly Eldorado for a
heavenly land of even greater riches that were their due.

They were men, in short, who believed they couldn't lose.
Such are invincible.

So the Conquistadores proved to be.

They were explorers who made exploring a career, and they
intended to make that career pay them handsomely. Some had
even more fanciful notions than finding Eldorado. Juan Ponce
de Leon, for one, was in no great hurry to arrive among the

heavenly elect. He sought the Fountain of Youth, a mythical spring left over from classical times, but now firmly planted in the New World. He reached that conclusion when he accompanied the new viceroy of Aragon and Castile to the New World on his second voyage. Columbus himself had more pressing matters to occupy his mind. But with Ponce de Leon that fountain, whose waters provided anyone who drank them with eternal youth, became a kind of personal *fata morgana*, luring him to explore new lands, always in the hope of discovering the elusive fountain. Seeking the fountain, he discovered what he at first thought was a new Carib island. Instead, it was a part of the North American mainland. Because of the blooms he discovered there he called the new land Florida.

That was in 1513. By this time the Conquistadores were becoming ambitious. Home in Spain young men dreamed of finding newer and richer native kingdoms. They thought little of crossing burning plains or climbing mountains capped with snow. The New World was theirs for the taking, and fresh lands were theirs for the discovering.

A constant stream of Eldorado seekers sailed westward, seekfame and fortune even when they had reservations about finding eternal youth. Such a Conquistadore was Vasco Nunez de Balboa. He had gone to the New World seeking fortune, but landing in Santo Domingo he had found only creditors, who pushed him hard for payment, and after escaping them as a stowaway in a barrel he joined an expedition setting out for Darien, otherwise the eastern part of Panama. There was so much gold in Darien, he had been told, that one had only to stoop to pick it out of the earth.

He and his companions with the gold fever set out in that same year that saw Ponce de Leon reach Florida. They had to cross a mountain range and endure considerable hardship and privation. But eventually, lured on by the hope of finding gold in abundance, they staggered across the isthmus and found a vast new ocean. Later Ferdinand Magellan was to give it a name after rounding the South American continent. Balboa merely called it the Southern Sea. He was a rather literal-minded explorer for all his golden illusions. He waded breast-high into this new sea, wearing his Conquistadore's armour and plumage.

' I claim this Southern Sea and all its shore and islands for

77

my sovereign lord the King of Spain,' he proclaimed grandilo-
quently.

He began men building a city. He had two Spanish ships
dragged over the mountains, so they could be sailed on this
Southern Sea. That was a stupendous feat. But Balboa like many
of his kind was quite capable of stupendous feats in that incredible age.

He sailed his new-found sea, exploring the coastline, and he
discovered the Pearl Islands in the Gulf of Panama. He continued almost to the coast of Peru. He was made governor of
the Darien colony he had founded. But his fortunes quickly
ebbed. He was replaced as governor by a man even more
avaricious, and one anxious to rid himself of a predecessor who
might prove dangerous. His name was Pedrarias Davila. Today
he is chiefly remembered as the man who imprisoned Balboa
who, to Davila's lordly mind, had gone native by marrying the
daughter of a local cacique or chieftain. Once having declared
himself as Balboa's enemy, Davila could not retreat from the
stand he had taken. He could only advance. He did this by
having Balboa beheaded. That was in 1517, as soon as he received news that Ferdinand was dead and had been succeeded
by Charles v. Ferdinand had no reason to agree to Balboa's
death, for the Conquistadore had once sent him fifteen thousand
crowns as a fifth share of some booty he had taken in warring
against the native chiefs. They happened to be the enemies of
his father-in-law.

Today the young man who came from the town of Xerez,
which gave its name to sherry, is remembered in the modern re-
public of Panama, for Balboa is the port of Panama City and
the country's chief coin is the balboa, roughly equivalent to an
American dollar.

It remains a perpetual pity that John Keats was so weak in
history as to confuse Balboa with Cortez. In his famous lines:

> ' Or like stout Cortez when with eagle eyes
> He star'd at the Pacific – and all his men
> Look'd at each other with a wild surmize –
> Silent, upon a peak in Darien '

the credit should have gone to Balboa, not to the conqueror of
Mexico.

. . . inflicted a gruelling defeat on the flower of Montezuma's army

79

Hernando Cortez was of course a contemporary of Balboa's who first set out for the New World in 1504. Two years after Balboa's head was severed from its trunk he marched overland against the Aztec empire of the proud Montezuma, whose capital was the fortress city of Mexico, built high in the mountains of the central mainland.

Cortez and his men performed great feats of valour and endured severe hardship in their driving quest to reach the capital of the Aztec empire. They began preparing to explore the mainland of Central America two years before, after learning from the natives of Yucatan that far to the west there was a fabulous city built in the middle of a high mountain lake. The people of this city had untold treasure.

That was enough to start the palms of the Spanish Eldorado seekers itching, and Cortez made a start by building a port on the coast as a base for the expedition he was to take exploring inland to find this Montezuma and his Aztec kingdom. He called the port Vera Cruz.

Finally in 1519 he started out with several hundred men, only a small proportion of whom were mounted, to conquer an empire and a civilization that had flourished for centuries. Cortez was the Conquistadore *par excellence*. No task was too great, no odds too intimidating. Personal discomfort was to be endured as a means to a great end.

The captains and soldiery accompanying Cortez had heard that the Aztecs were a cruel people dominated by a priesthood that demanded numerous human sacrifices, especially maidens. The Aztec culture had developed a picturesque form of picture-writing, and the men were brave and skilled in war, for they had conquered such important tribes as the Tlascalans and virtually made them into serfs to work their mines and fields. Moreover, under Montezuma II they had extended their sovereignty to Honduras and Nicaragua, and stories of the Aztec emperor's despotism and cruelty had extended throughout Central America. Cortez and his men considered they would be warring against forces of evil when they reached Tenochtitlan, as Montezuma called his lake island palace fort where today Mexico City stands.

However, Cortez, like Balboa a few years before, had his administrative troubles. He was angered by the demands made upon him by Velasquez, the Governor of Cuba, and when he had built his port of Vera Cruz on the mainland he suddenly issued a proclamation, in which he renounced all personal allegiance to Velasquez, declaring himself to own from henceforth allegiance only to the King of Spain.

It was a bold move, and one calculated to have repercussions later, but Cortez was a very bold man and audacious as well. He shrewdly contended that, if he returned a conqueror from his march against Montezuma, bearing great treasure to share with his Royal master in Seville, then he would have little to fear from a mere colonial governor.

So the famous march into the interior began. It proved to be one of the most spectacular undertaken by a sword-in-hand explorer bent on conquering what he discovered. The well-armed and disciplined Spaniards put to flight the trained bands of Tlascalans and inflicted a gruelling defeat on the flower of Montezuma's army. On 8 November 1519, Cortez entered Tenochtitlan at the head of his army, and Montezuma II, the proud despot, became a captive in the hands of his conquerors.

It has been said that the Aztecs put up no spirited resistance to the Spaniards because their priests had told them that one day a great god would come to them from the east, and to their superstitious eyes Hernando Cortez more than filled the role, especially with his mounted troops, who appeared to the Aztecs to be half men, half horse, creatures who struck mortal fear into Montezuma's warriors by their very appearance. The Aztecs had no cavalry, and could not conceive of such troops being normal human beings.

Moreover, although the Aztecs were warriors, they had a curious reluctance to kill their enemies in conflict. They preferred to take them prisoner and afterwards hand them over to the priests to be sacrificed to the gods they worshipped.

With Montezuma deposed, his own people turned against the royal captive of the Spaniards. Because he wished to be conciliatory after winning so great a victory Cortez presented the turquoise-crowned Montezuma to those among his nobles who would destroy him. The wretched emperor's body fell festooned with Aztec arrows, and day's later he died like a weary animal in a dark corner of his looted palace.

Cortez felt it necessary to start back to Vera Cruz, but he

dispatched some of his captains with troops to explore westward and to the north. Some of them eventually reached the Pacific and pushed into California and Texas. The Conquistadores were really spreading across America like a stain. For two years the soldiers of Cortez explored and plundered their military way over the land.

Meanwhile Cortez had to deal with Diego de Velasquez, whose private secretary he had once been, for the Governor of Cuba had dispatched a punitive expedition to the mainland to deal with the upstart. This comprised no less than nineteen ships with nine hundred men and twenty cannon. So the conquest of Mexico was halted for vital months while Cortez marched post-haste for the coast in May 1520, with two hundred and sixty of his veterans. He now proved that he could win against Spanish arms as decisively as he had against the *maquahuitls*, or obsidian swords, and arrows of the Aztecs. In a midnight battle fought in a tropical downpour on Whit Monday Cortez and his men, after their long march from the mountains, defeated five times their number, and when the battle was over most of Velasquez's men deserted to join Cortez, who made an about-turn and marched back to complete the subjugation of the Aztecs at the head of a thousand infantry, nearly a hundred cavalry, and almost the same number of both crossbow men and arquebusiers.

After a hero's return to Spain he sailed again to the New World, and for ten years from 1530 devoted his energies to exploring Mexico and the lands around. He returned finally to Spain in 1540, and seven years later, aged sixty-three, suffering from dysentery and still dreaming of Eldorado, he died in Seville, the most renowned of the Conquistadores. However, he died comforted by the knowledge that he had fired with zeal Francisco Pizarro, who was to emulate Cortez's example in Peru, where he was to bring the Inca kingdom and civilization under Spanish dominion just as Cortez had brought those of the Aztecs.

Pizarro, however, fought under less favourable stars than the conqueror of Montezuma and Mexico. He was the illegitimate son of a landed Spaniard. He went to the New World with the golden Eldorado glint in his dark eyes and found status by selling his services to Balboa. He heard the traveller's tales

about a land called Biru, or Peru, and set out with some companions to reconnoitre the country in 1528. Word was sent after
him from Panama's Governor to return, whereupon Pizarro is
said to have drawn his sword and made a line running east and
west on the sand where he stood.

'To the south, comrades-in-arms,' he said, 'lies the way of
hardship. We shall end it in Peru, but we shall be rich.' His
sword pointed northwards. 'There lies Panama and poverty.
The choice is ours.'

As he finished speaking he stepped to the south of the line
he had drawn, and thirteen of his companions stepped with him.
They were to be the leaders of the conquerors of Peru and the
Inca nation.

Pizarro had come up the hard way, as we say today, and he
knew he had defied Pedro de los Rios, the Panama Governor,
though not as flagrantly as Cortez had defied Diego de Velasquez. But he was anxious not to earn the trouble Cortez had to
overcome, so he boldly returned to Spain with his close companion Pedro de Candia, and they took with them objects of
gold and silver and cloth made of vicuna wool, which closely
resembled silk. Candia had a tongue more golden than any
object presented to the court gathering in Toledo, and spun such
a fanciful story of the treasure to be obtained in Peru that
Pizarro had little persuading to do. The royal ears were well
cocked and the royal palms itched pleasantly.

Pizarro and his original thirteen companions were made
hidalgos, or noblemen, by royal decree, and he sailed again for
the New World with Candia. An expedition was fitted out to
move against the Inca ruler, Atahualpa. In three ships the
Eldorado seekers under Pizarro sailed from Panama in January
1531. In their company was Pizarro's own half-brother
Hernando, born legitimately and brought up at court, who
was to be the official spokesman for the conquerors in treating
with Atahualpa when they reached his stronghold of Cajamarca.
This advance was made after gruelling progress over mountains
and through dense jungles, only for the Inca king to reject the
opportunity to become a vassal of Charles v.

With a few hand-picked companions, and yelling, 'St James
and at them!' Pizarro dashed forward with drawn sword, and
Atahualpa was prisoner before the first of the Spanish cannon

thundered. When they did, and after the bugles had sounded the charge, four thousand Incas were slaughtered in less than half an hour. At the end of that time Charles v had a fresh empire to send him a ceaseless flow of tribute.

Pizarro's secretary, Francisco de Xerez, relates how the captive Inca ruler, realizing how the Spaniards worshipped gold, bargained for his freedom :

'He asked to be led before Pizarro and offered to fill the room in which he was captured with gold as high as he could reach with his fingertips, if the Spaniard would give him his freedom in return. Pizarro then asked how much time he would need for this and Atahualpa replied, " Two months." The Governor accepted this offer and told Atahualpa that if he kept his promise he need fear nothing.'

But Pizarro was a liar and a cheat, spoiled rotten by the wealth of the land in which he found himself conqueror, a land where horseshoes were made of solid silver because it had no iron. Atahualpa had the room filled as he promised, and that room of seventeen feet by twenty-two was choked with gold to the agreed height several days short of the two months. But the captive was given a sword thrust instead of his freedom.

Atahualpa's murder was a deed of folly. Pizarro plundered the rich city of Cuzco, but he soon had an uprising to deal with. His method of doing so can be expressed in one word – massacre. But while most of the Conquistadores in Peru continued their grim routine of pillage and plunder some, still seeking their own private Eldorado, set out on fresh journeys of exploration. They roved down into Chile, fighting Indian tribes and disease, others crawled like metalled ants over the Andes to reach Bolivia and the silver-mines of Potosi. Francisco de Orellana broke away from an expedition that seven months before had set out from Quito to try to find the Atlantic, and reached a tributary stream that eventually led him to a mighty watercourse, where he heard of female warriors called the Coniupuara, who were said to be led by a chieftainess named Conori.

Orellana and his companions finally reached the Atlantic on 11 September 1542. They had journeyed more than two thousand five hundred miles in two hundred and sixty days. Orellana, like many Conquistadores before him, sailed for Spain to report his discoveries in person, and then returned to South America. With five hundred men he set out through the Amazon jungle, still seeking Eldorado. He did not return to report again. He vanished without trace, in 1545.

By that time Francisco Pizarro was a polluted memory in the land he had conquered. In the summer of 1541 he had been assassinated by the friends of Diego de Almagro, who had rebelled against him and later been strangled in his prison cell after being defeated before the city of Cuzco.

It was rumoured Atahualpa, just before he was murdered, cursed both of them. Death hung like a dark pall over the golden trails blazed by the armour-clad explorers of Spain.

TO THE LAND OF THE GREAT BEAR

In 1518 a Spanish caravel, sailing from Haiti to Puerto Rico, saw a vessel that did not fly the standard of St James. Sunlight winked from the cannon on its deck. More curious than alarmed, the Spaniards lowered a boat and rowed over to the strange ship.

She was English, and her captain said he had been sailing with another craft that had become separated from him during a great storm. He had found himself drifting through a sea dotted with giant ice floes, so he had turned south, intending to make for Brazil. He had reached Puerto Rico.

'Where were you heading for when you set out?' he was asked.

'The land of the Great Cham,' he told the Spaniards.

Obviously he had been trying the northern route found by John Cabot. Eventually he reached Santo Domingo, to find himself covered by the fort's guns, which promptly fired on the English intruder, for the sudden appearance of the stranger had alarmed Francisco de Tapia, the governor, so much he almost panicked. Disgruntled by such unfriendly treatment, the English captain turned his ship around and departed. He arrived back in Puerto Rico, where he exchanged some of his cargo of wrought iron, which was doubtless intended for the yellow-faced subjects of the Great Cham, for fresh supplies of food and drinking water, and then sailed back to England.

As for the inhospitable de Tapia, he was strongly criticized for not having captured the intruder, because it was realized others would follow, as indeed they did, men like Tom Tyson, a bluff English sea captain who took his ship to the West Indies in 1526 to trade on behalf of a group of English merchants, and was prepared to fight if he had to, which events proved to be no unnecessary precaution.

French and Dutch ships sailed the same sea lanes as the English. What began as trading ventures became warlike excursions that led in the result to outright piracy.

This was not the end desired by the more forward-thinking merchants in London and Bristol and other English ports. While they wanted trade on favourable terms with Spaniards or Portuguese if these could be obtained, they also sought new routes to fresh sources of trade. Above all they still wanted their own trade routes to Cathay by way of what was termed the Northwest Passage through the American land mass. To find these routes they were prepared to defray the expenses of expeditions to explore the northern sea lanes.

They were, to a large extent, led to such a decision by a certain Robert Thorne, who had been born in Bristol, had lived in Seville, and had settled upon his return to England in London. In 1513, realizing the divided state of the explored world, he composed what has been described as a declaration. He had the temerity to address it Henry viii. It opened its argument by pointing out:

' Of the four parts of the world it seemeth three parts are discovered by other Princes. For out of Spain they have discovered all the Indies and Seas Occidental, and out of Portugal all the Indies and Seas Oriental: so that by this part of the Orient and Occident they have compassed the world.'

Master Thorne went on to point out a few other harsh facts of sixteenth-century life, and then said succinctly, ' So there now rest to be discovered the said North parts, the which, it seemeth to me, is only your charge and duty.'

Whatever Henry viii thought about such a declaration, its terms as well as its implication, were accepted by the merchants of London, for in 1517 a certain gentleman with the somewhat forbidding name of Sir Thomas Pert set out to find the Northwest Passage that had become a topic of conversation where men with a taste for exploration commingled. It is thought Sebastian Cabot might have sailed with him. They had no success. Nor did certain other English venturers upon the Northern main. Just about the time they may have been growing dispirited Master Thorne came up with another thought-provoking composition. This was in 1527.

He reminded thinking Englishmen that the Spaniards had the westward route to the Orient by the Strait of Magellan, first reported in Europe five years before, when the *Vittoria* arrived home under the command of Sebastian del Cano, and the Portuguese had the eastward route discovered by da Gama. He pointed out that only the North-west and North-east Passages remained for the English to find and so reach the lands of great trading wealth. These constituted what he termed a third way. He wrote:

'And if they go this third way, and after they be past the Pole, go right towards the Pole Antarctic, and then decline towards the lands and islands situated between the tropics, and under the equinoctial, without doubt they shall find there the richest lands and islands of the world, of gold, precious stones, balms, spices, and other things that we here esteem most, which come out of strange countries; and may return the same way.'

Master Thorne still had considerable powers of persuasion, but little beyond mere theory to back them up. While his theory was debated a Breton seaman named Jacques Cartier reached the Belle Isle Strait, between Newfoundland and Labrador, in 1534, and the next year, again sailing this strait, reached the mouth of the St Lawrence, which he sailed up as far as a town occupied by friendly redmen. They called their town of tepees and wigwams Hochelaga. Today the site is covered by Montreal. Cartier and his men wintered near the site of present-day Quebec. He called this land Canada, which was the redman's word for an Indian village. On his way back to France he found a broader straight than Belle Isle. Today it is marked Cabot Strait on the maps of Canada.

However, by the time Sebastian Cabot returned to England from the Continent, in 1548, the North-west Passage was somewhat out of favour due largely to repeated failures to find it, and merchants and seamen were considering more hopefully the concept of a North-east Passage, spoken of so assuringly by

Master Thorne. They consulted Sebastian Cabot, and he was at once enthusiastic about the possibilities of finding such a passage, and even agreed to head a company of merchant adventurers who were prepared to fit out ships to venture to the north-east, find the passage, sail through it, and reach Cathay by the back door.

Three ships were prepared in due course, fitted with armour and armaments, victualled for eighteen months' sailing, and put under the command of Sir Hugh Willoughby, with Richard Chancellor as his second in command. The ships were the *Edward Bonaventure*, the *Bona Speranza,* and the *Confidentia.* They sailed from London on 10 May 1553, cleared the Thames and reached Harwich, where they were delayed by contrary winds until 23 June, when they finally headed into the North Sea and lost sight of the English coast.

We know from Willoughby's journal that the three ships duly reached the Lofoten Islands, where they remained at anchor for some days. Afterwards they were separated by a storm accompanied by fog when they continued their voyage north, and although Willoughby and his men reached the mouth of the Arzina River in Lapland it was merely to endure a bitingly cold winter with provisions running low and finally to succumb to sub-zero temperatures and frost-bite.

Meantime, Chancellor, now on his own, was faced by the alternative of continuing as originally planned or turning back for England. He went on to Vardo, in Norway, where well-intentioned folk tried to dissuade him from the more hazardous course. But Chancellor was a dogged man, and one not lightly turned from his purpose. As Clement Adams, who sailed with him in the *Edward Bonaventure,* relates in an account of the journey written in Latin, Chancellor sailed on until he came at last to the places where he found no night at all, but a continual light and brightness of the sun shining clearly upon the huge and mighty sea.'

Chancellor, in short, was sailing under the midnight sun. ' And having the benefit of this perpetual light for certain days,' Adams continued, ' at length it pleased God to bring them to a certain great bay, which was of a hundred miles or thereabouts over.'

He had now reached the shore of the White Sea, where he

found some fishermen who bowed low before him and attempted to kiss his feet. Chancellor learned that he had reached the land of Muscovy, which was vast and ruled over by a certain Juan Vasilivich. In history this ruler has been accorded the name he earned by his deeds, Ivan the Terrible.

Muscovites who came to visit the Englishmen asked the name of the ruler of the land from which they had sailed. They were told King Edward VI, and Chancellor managed to make them understand that his object in coming was to deliver to their king certain gifts from his, and to trade and express their friendship for the people of Muscovy.

After a good deal of argument and not a little misunderstanding, Chancellor and his party set out on sleighs across the frozen steppes, a wasteland that is, as Adams put it, ' congealed in the winter-time by the force of the cold, which in those places is very extreme and horrible '. They were met by a messenger from the Tsar, who arranged for post-horses to be supplied to the Englishmen, and the long journey of some fifteen hundred miles continued until at last Richard Chancellor stood in a city of strange barbaric splendour which he was told was called Moscow.

Twelve days after the arrival of the English party in the capital of Ivan the Terrible the Tsar sent for Chancellor, who later gave his own impressions in a book he published on his return to England :

' When the Duke was in his place appointed, an interpreter came for me into the outer chamber, where sat one hundred or more gentlemen, all in cloth of gold very sumptuous, and from thence I came into the council chamber, where sat the Duke himself with his nobles, which were a fair company : they sat round about the chamber on high, yet so that he himself sat much higher than any of his nobles in a chair gilt, and in a long garment of beaten gold, with an imperial crown upon his head, and a staff of crystal and gold in his right hand, and his other hand half-leaning on his chair.'

A letter Chancellor had brought from Edward VI was duly delivered and he was invited to dinner with Ivan, whom he refers to constantly in his narrative as the Duke of Muscovia. ' Also,' he comments with surprise, ' before dinner he changed

*. . . a city of strange barbaric splendour which he was told was
Moscow*

his crown, and in dinner-time two crowns; so that I saw three separate crowns upon his head in one day.'

Now that he had reached the Land of the Great Bear the Englishman Richard Chancellor was a keen observer of customs and life. He was amazed to learn that when Ivan the Terrible put himself at the head of an army to begin a campaign it seldom numbered less than two hundred thousand troops. When Ivan went to war he was arrayed as though for a fête. ' His pavilion is covered either with cloth of gold or silver,' Chancellor tells us, ' and so set with stones that it is wonderful to see. I have seen the King's Majesty of England,' he adds wistfully, ' and the French King's pavilions, which are fair, yet not like unto his.'

He thought little of the Russian soldiers' discipline, but thought that, properly trained, they would prove great fighters. He had no great esteem for the judicial system he found operating, and when he learned that the poor existed on a diet of parings and stinking fish he understood something told him by one of the Muscovites he met :

' I heard a Russian say that it was a great deal merrier living in prison than forth, but for the great beating. For they have meat and drink without labour, and get the charity of well-disposed people : but being at liberty they get nothing.'

In the Land of the Great Bear living for the serfs was several hundred years behind the times as expressed in conditions enjoyed by English labourers and peasants in the mid-sixteenth century.

Such feudal conditions were to continue largely unchanged for a further three centuries.

Chancellor had not found a North-east Passage and he had not found a route to Cathay, but when he started on his return journey in 1554 he carried with him a letter from Tsar Ivan to King Edward VI that was virtually a trade agreement between the two countries. By its terms English merchants were promised a free and welcome market for all their goods throughout the Land of the Great Bear.

Not until he arrived back in England did Chancellor discover that he was no longer the subject of a king, but of a queen. Edward VI had died in the previous year, and Queen Mary reigned, a monarch far more concerned with her subjects' religious beliefs than their genius for trading. The daughter of Catherine of Aragon married Philip of Spain, and before she died lost the last English toe-hold on the European mainland, Calais, and earned a reputation for violence that brought her the descriptive title of Bloody Mary.

In the following year the Muscovy Company of Merchant Adventurers, founded in 1553 to further the exploratory voyage by Willoughby and Chancellor, received a charter from Queen Mary, while the Rusian Tsar granted them special privileges in a document which named 'Sebastian Cabota' as governor of the company. In the next year, 1556, Stephen Burrough, who had been master of the *Edward Bonaventure,* set out to search for the *Bona Speranza* and *Confidentia,* and on his way explored the area of the Obi River. The year was not over before the first Russian ambassador to England sailed in the *Edward Bonaventure* with Chancellor to arrange a diplomatic link between the courts of Terrible Ivan and Bloody Mary.

The ship foundered and Chancellor was lost, but the Russian ambassador was saved to reach London, where he was given a civic reception and made to feel he was truly among friends. When he sailed back to Russian in a ship modestly named *Primrose* he was accompanied by four other vessels laden with trade goods.

The days of the monopoly of the Hanseatic League in the Baltic were over. The League might retain its Staple-House in Novgorod, but Russia's very wide back door was open to the English. It was still open in the mid-twentieth century when fresh Hanseatic rivals blocked the Baltic gateway. History, as students of it are constantly discovering, is seldom shy of repeating itself.

Bold men still sought the North-east Passage, but after Stephen Burrough returned from exploring the coastline of Nova Zembla one man had the notion of trying to reach Cathay by a northern overland route through Russia. This was Anthony Jenkinson, who started to blaze a fresh trail and actually got as far as Bokhara in 1558.

Cathay, the Far East, the Spice Islands, the domain of the Grand Cham – all remained as remote to the English of the mid-sixteenth century as they had to the navigators of Portugal when

Prince Henry was trying to revolutionize their outlook and technique.

Nineteen years after Jenkinson came to a halt in Bokhara Sir Humphrey Gilbert wrote a discourse in which he referred to the voyage made by Othere to the White Sea and pointed out that this was the same route currently used by English traders sailing to Muscovy on regular annual voyages. He pointed out that Chancellor had actually rediscovered the route, and admitted that if any sea captain had sailed for Muscovy by Othere's route, relying upon King Alfred's narrative, he would have been thought mad.

Yet, he emphasized, Othere had spoken no less than the truth. The way to the White Sea did exist, and it was a route for traders to follow.

All of which was merely an argument to emphasize something else – namely, that there must surely be a North-west Passage to Cathay. It merely had still to be found. Gilbert argued that the existence of such a sea passage was believed by the most renowned geographers, ancient and modern.

When that discourse appeared in print it was like a new edition of Master Thorne's writings of fifty years before. Men who still wanted adventure with profit and perhaps even fame suddenly refurbished all the old arguments and claims for the existence of the North-west Passage.

The North-east Passage was no longer a fashionable topic. The North-west Passage was back in favour. It remained in favour, on and off, until it was eventually found.

By which time it had largely lost its original meaning and certainly offered no competitive route to those explored by da Gama and Magellan.

THE LURE OF THE NORTH-WEST
PASSAGE

W H A T had stimulated Sir Humphrey Gilbert to write his famous *Discourse of a Discovery of a New Passage to Cathay* was the intrepid searching by another English mariner of the period, Sir Martin Frobisher. Elizabeth, Mary's half-sister, was on the throne, and England was again a Protestant country. Her brother-in-law, Philip of Spain, alternately railed against her and tried to cajole her, but she held him in contempt and was not afraid to show it. English adventurers took their cue from the queen. The Spaniards and their treasure fleets from the Indies and the Americas were sailing the Spanish Main, it would seem, for the prime purpose of being harried by the English.

The Dutch and the French had much the same idea, but because Philip had been married to Queen Mary he was held in very special loathing by the vast majority of Elizabeth's countrymen. Some endeavoured to steal a march on the Spanish sea captains. Martin Frobisher was one, Francis Drake another. Frobisher went seeking the north-west route to Cathay, Drake went south and west in the wake of Magellan. They went sailing on their voyages of exploration and profit at the same time. At least, Frobisher made three distinct voyages in 1576, 1577, and 1578. Drake's voyage round the world was made between 1577 and 1580, and during it he discovered an island he named for his queen.

When Captain Martin Frobisher sailed in search of the North-west Passage on his first voyage of exploration, in 1576, he was no knight. His prowess in the battle against the Armada

95

won him the knightly accolade twelve years later. He was a bluff Yorkshireman who could handle men and ships, and when he was offered a commission in 1575 by the Muscovy Company to go in search of a North-west Passage to India he agreed to accept it. He was given two ships, the *Gabriel* and the *Michael,* each of only thirty tons, and a pinnace of ten tons, for his command, and on May 8th, in the next year, he sailed down the Thames. He was something of a showman, for as he passed the royal palace he dressed his craft with bunting and fired a salute. Elizabeth appeared at an open window and waved to the departing seamen.

Frobisher headed for the Shetlands and at last reached Greenland, where he ran into squally weather that was too much for the pinnace, which sank. When the other two ships became separated the *Michael's* captain turned for home. It wasn't a brave decision, but it was undoubtedly a wise one. Frobisher in the *Gabriel* sailed on into a sea where icebergs dwarfed his modest craft. He kept a westerly course until he sighted land known today as Baffin Island, sighted six hundred years before by the Viking crew of Bjarni Herjulfson. He found a wide bay which he thought wrongly was a strait, and he explored it to discover 'whether I might carry myself through to the back side'.

Today we know this inlet as Frobisher Bay. On its shores Frobisher and his men sighted Eskimos, and Kit Hall, the *Gabriel's* master, wrote :

'They be like to Tartars, with long black hair, broad faces and flat noses, tawny in colour, wearing sealskins, and so do the women, not differing in the fashion, but the women are marked in the face with blue streaks in the cheeks and round the eyes. Their boats are made all of seals' skins with a keel of wood between the skin.'

When he was certain he had found a bay and not a strait, and so had not discovered the North-west Passage, Frobisher returned to the Thames.

Seven months later he was northward-bound again, with a larger squadron, comprising the two angelically named ships, the *Gabriel* and the *Michael*, the *Aide*, and a number of pinnaces. He reached Frobisher Bay by July, when he went ashore, claimed the land for Queen Elizabeth, and unfurled the standard of St George. The land was formally named Meta Incognita. Again he did not find a through seaway, but when he returned to England he brought some ore samples that contained flecks of gold. New dreams of Eldorado sent him back to Meta Incongnita with a fleet of no less than sixteen ships and provisions for spending a winter in the Arctic. They named a part of the Greenland shore West of England and one particular cliff Charing Cross. A storm cost him five ships and some of his vital winter supplies. He reached Hudson Strait and went up it for sixty miles before discontent among his anxious crews forced him to turn back. He sailed back to England where the news awaited him that his ore samples had not contained gold, but merely iron pyrites, the fool's gold of prospectors in every gold rush since men became greedy for the colourful metal.

The disappointed Frobisher, who was later to sail with Drake to the West Indies, had advanced the sum total of knowledge about the northern seas. He had proved a vast archipelago sprawled to the extreme north of the Americas.

In the year of Frobisher's third and last voyage in search of the elusive sea passage Humphrey Gilbert, the author of the *Discourse,* sold his land and home to raise money to stock a fresh expedition. It was dogged by ill-luck, and Gilbert put off his next attempt to cross the Atlantic and start exploring until 1583, when he set out from England with five ships, including the *Delight* and the *Raleigh,* named for his stepbrother. The *Raleigh* was the largest vessel, but when her captain and many of her crew were laid low by a mysterious illness Gilbert doggedly continued in the *Delight,* accompanied by the tiny *Squirrel* of ten tons and the *Swallow* and *Golden Hind* of forty tons. This *Golden Hind,* of course, was not Drake's famous ship of the same name. Off the Newfoundland coast rough weather caused the *Delight* to lose contact with the *Swallow* and *Squirrel,* but the four ships came together again in the Bay of St John. Gilbert landed people he had brought across the Atlantic to found a colony, and he formally took possession of Newfoundland in the name of Queen Elizabeth and set up the English coat of arms ' engraved in lead and set upon a pillar of wood '.

The colony started badly. Some of the colonists displayed

a greater interest in piracy than in manual work, and Gilbert had plenty of trouble before he decided it was time to start back for England. He sailed in the little *Squirrel* after refusing to transfer aboard the *Golden Hind*. The *Delight* had been wrecked, while the *Swallow* had returned to England with the numerous sick members of the expedition.

Gilbert told Captain Hayes of the *Golden Hind*, 'I will not forsake my little company going homeward, with whom I have passed so many storms and perils.' But the two vessels ran into mountainous seas. Sir Humphrey Gilbert was observed seated in a chair in the small stern reading a book. Again Hayes pleaded with him to come aboard the larger vessel. Gilbert looked up from his book, and shouted, 'We are as near heaven by sea as by land!'

Dark came down, lanterns were hung in the rigging, but by midnight the *Golden Hind* had the Atlantic to herself. The little *Squirrel* had foundered, taking to the grey-green depths the brave man who had founded the first English colony.

By this time the Dutch were not only following the English to the West Indies, but sailing north to find their own sea passages, and in 1596 one of them, William Barentz, on his third voyage, took a more northerly course and reached Bear Island. He continued to Spitzbergen, which he mistakenly thought was Greenland, then turned east, got caught in the pack ice, and his crew had to endure an Arctic winter. They fed on the flesh of bears and foxes and used the skins for clothing. Only a few of them returned safely to Holland. Barentz himself died in the wasteland he had found and explored, Novaya Zemlya, or Nova Zembla.

Henry Hudson was a British seaman who sailed to find first the North-east Passage to Cathay, and later the North-west Passage to the same elusive land. He was supported in his efforts by the Muscovy Company and the newly formed Dutch East Company, and although he failed he brought back a great deal of polar information that was of great value and assistance to whalers. In 1610, on his second voyage west and a year after he had discovered the Hudson River, he sailed into Hudson Bay, seeking the North-west Passage, but was trapped by winter when it closed down on his ship with an iron grip. He and his crew had a bad time, for the Eskimos were not friendly and their

*. . . got caught in the pack ice, and his crew had to endure an
Arctic winter*

food gave out, leaving them to exist on a thin diet of moss and frogs. They said the moss and lichens were worse to eat than sawdust.

He tried to continue again that summer, but his crew mutinied as another winter approached and they cast Hudson, his nineteen-year-old son, and some sick sailors adrift in a small boat. What happened to the castaway left in the great bay named after him is not known.

A few years later William Baffin was off to search for the North-west Passage. He pinned his hopes of being successful to continuing up Davis Strait. This strait had been named for another Devon man, like Gilbert. John Davis had felt the lure of the mysterious sea passage, and in 1585 and the two following years had made three dogged attempts to reach it by probing deep between Baffin Land and Greenland, and reaching farther north than his predecessors. He found the Eskimos he met friendly. During the time he spent among these northern nomads he taught them to play football. He did not find the passage, and returned with his holds full of fish and sealskins instead of gold and spices. But he was more convinced of the existence of the North-west Passage than before he had sailed north.

That was the kind of lure the sea passage had for seamen of this time, and Baffin, who followed Davis, was no exception. He pushed farther north even than Davis, keeping westerly between Greenland and Labrador up through Davis Strait and reached the great sea called Baffin Bay. He sailed up inlets now named Jones and Lancaster Sounds, but found his way blocked. He had made valuable explorations, but he had not found the North-west Passage.

By this time merchants in England had other conceptions to occupy their minds. Sir Humphrey Gilbert's Newfoundland experiment in colonizing was followed by Sir Walter Raleigh's founding of a colony in Virginia. Money for voyages of mere exploration began to be hard for mariners to come by, and after Baffin had returned to England and given his opinion that he did not think the passage would be found anywhere south of where he had sailed even the hardiest of believers felt some of the old-time lure fading.

Besides, men like Davis, who knew the northern seas, after several failures had been content to head for the West Indies, where there was always a Spanish treasure ship or two to be challenged.

In fact, the lure of the North-west Passage was not felt as a challenge men could not resist until another two centuries had passed, and then it was not trade that turned men's eyes towards the Arctic, but science and a desire to know more about the physical nature of the world in which we live.

So a new phase in searching for the North-west Passage commenced when in 1818 John Ross and W. E. Parry set out on what today we would call a polar expedition. They reached Lancaster Sound, where Ross decided progress at this point was not possible, and the trip was called off. However, the next year he returned with two vessels and more supplies, and he continued through Lancaster Sound and on through Barrow Strait to Melville Island, where winter came down and the explorers had to make camp. Scurvy was the age-old danger, and this was held at bay when Parry began growing mustard and cress in the warmth of the stove-pipe in his cabin. Parry was, in a sense, the epitome of the new breed of explorer attracted to the icy seas in an age that was feeling the growing benefits of the Industrial Revolution, and could look back on the development of colonial settlements in the sixteenth century and the explorations of men like Captain James Cook in the seventeenth, and the discovery of many new lands, including the new continent comprising Australia and New Zealand.

William Edward Parry had entered the Royal Navy the year after Trafalgar, and with the close of the Napoleonic Wars he was, like a good many other well-trained naval officers, looking for something that offered the spice of adventure and a challenge to his intelligence.

Like John Ross, he found that challenge in the Arctic seas. He also found more than just a spice of adventure. Throughout that winter of 1819 he not only grew mustard and cress to provide fresh greenstuff for his men, but he organized amateur theatricals for the evenings and exploring parties for the daytime. In between times he edited a news-sheet for the expedition's members. He called it *The North Georgian Gazette*.

It was probably in the moments of musing while writing his regular piece for the news-sheet that he came to the conclusion that they might be aiming too far to the north, whereas the chances of finding the centuries-sought passage would be better to the south, where the winters were less ironbound.

However that may be, two years later, in 1821, Parry headed back to the Arctic shores and tundras and began exploring to the north-west of that great inland sea, Hudson Bay. He had to spend another winter in the Arctic, but by this time he was a veteran and not easily daunted by the long northern nights, and when spring started breaking the ice he continued north through Fox Channel, and came to discover a narrow strip of sea between Baffin Island and Canada proper. He took his two ships down the length of this strait and named it after them. The ships were the *Hecla* and the *Fury*.

The lure of those northern seaways that he had first felt in the years between 1811 and 1813, when he was a naval officer engaged on protective patrols to safeguard the whalers of Spitzbergen, grew with each voyage he made to try to find the Northwest Passage, and in 1824 he was again in Arctic waters, this time nosing north of Baffin Island and through the newly discovered waterway named Prince Regent Inlet. But this time he not only failed to find the passage he still sought with a growing desperation, but the *Fury* was wrecked.

He should have been thoroughly discouraged. Perhaps he was. If so, then his last attempt to find the North-west Passage might be considered the peak of his career's achievement. It was made after another lapse of two years, in 1827, and when he returned his log-book showed that he had this time reached a record latitude of eighty-two degrees, forty-five minutes North.

It was a record that stood unbeaten by any other explorer for fifty years. Upon his return to England he was knighted. In 1821 he had written a book entitled *Voyages to the North-west Passage*. Unfortunately the hopeful title was not truly justified.

But while Parry was testing himself and his ideas against the Arctic on his second voyage another explorer was trying to obtain the same objective, the North-west Passage, by a most hazardous overland route.

His name was John Franklin. Like Parry, he had been a naval officer, and had fought with Nelson at the battle of Copenhagen. Like Ross and Parry, too, he had been attracted by the reward offered by Sir John Barrow, Secretary to the Admiralty, for the discovery of the North-west Passage, and again like them, he felt a personal challenge and was a man with a love of adventuring and pitting himself against the unknown.

Actually there were two Arctic explorers in the first part of the nineteenth century named Ross. John Ross and his nephew James, who became even more famous than the uncle. Both were eventually knighted for their services to science, and both sailed on voyages with Parry. John Ross discovered Boothia Land after a voyage on which he had trouble with the engines of his paddle steamer, for he had had the novel idea of taking a steamship to the Arctic. He set out on sledge to find why a compass does not point to true north. However, it remained for nephew James Clark to find and reach the North Magnetic Pole in 1831. He proudly hoisted the Union Jack over it. On this memorable expedition the explorers had to abandon a ship held unrelently in the pack ice, and when they trudged away another flag was left lying in the bitter Arctic air that froze men's breath before their faces. They actually reached the piled-up wreck of the *Fury*, which had been abandoned earlier by Parry, and removed the stores still in her hold. Had the *Fury* not awaited them they might never have returned, for those explorers spent four harsh winters in the Arctic before, half-dead from their privations, they were picked up by a whaler.

That expedition, which John Franklin might have looked upon as a premonition for himself, is generally termed the Booth Expedition because on it the Ross uncle and nephew not only found the North Magnetic Pole, but discovered the Arctic peninsular in which it was located, which they named Boothia Land or Boothia Felix, as they named a gulf some sixty to a hundred miles wide the Gulf of Boothia, after their patron who sponsored the expedition, Sir Felix Booth.

Franklin and James Clark Ross were explorers whose names became identified with the age-long search for the North-west Passage, but they were men whose careers took them into both northern and southern hemispheres, and curiously they were in each hemisphere at the same time as one another. When Franklin was Governor of Van Diemen's Land, as Tasmania was called then, James Ross set out with two ships, the *Erebus* and the *Terror*, on an Anarctic expedition that discovered Victoria Land and Mount Erebus and on which Ross made the first successful ocean sounding with a special plumb-line he had made for the purpose, which reached a depth of 14,550 feet. Today the Ross Sea and Ross Island in the Antarctic are named after him.

Again Franklin might be forgiven for having some presentiment when he heard of Ross's ships, the *Erebus* and the *Terror*. His own life was to be shaped by them, as was his death.

On that earlier overland expedition, made at the time of Parry's second voyage, Franklin crossed northern Canada from Hudson Bay to Lake Athabasca, and in his anxiety to reach the Coppermine River met misfortune and was saved from total disaster by the heroism of a single man, George Back, who made a journey on snowshoes of over a thousand miles to bring help and succour. Even then Franklin went on to Coronation Gulf and the self-explanatory Turnagain Point. The hardships endured by the party evoked Parry's admiration for such undaunted explorers.

Again they were truly undaunted. Franklin went again with such men as George Back and John Richardson to the Canadian snowlands, and while the main party wintered on the Great Bear Lake the leader himself pressed on down the Mackenzie River. Again bad weather interfered with carefully laid plans, but these explorers succeeded in surveying more than a thousand miles of some of the toughest coastline in the world.

It was after returning from Tasmania that Franklin, a man approaching sixty, but as undaunted as ever, decided to make a fresh attempt to find the North-west Passage. His earlier Arctic exploits had earned him a knighthood. Now he was to prove it had not been lightly bestowed.

He was provided with the two ships, *Erebus* and *Terror,* that Sir James Ross had brought home from the Antarctic, and in 1845 he sailed in high hopes of achieving what had been his dream and his ambition, the discovery of the North-west Passage. which was in fact to cost him his life.

The two ill-fated exploration ships were last sighted in Baffin Bay. Today it is generally accepted that an inaccurate chart of the period, showing King William Island joined to Boothia Felix, instead of being separated by James Ross Strait, caused Franklin to decide on going through Victoria Strait, to the west, and here his ships became trapped in the ice. The only positive recourse was to make another overland journey, and in company with his Eskimos he and his party set out, presumably to die of starvation and fall in their tracks.

Years later, after the Norwegian explorer, Roald Amundsen, in his exploration ship the *Gjoa*, of only forty-seven tons and seventy feet long, and so comparable to some of the ships of Sir Humphrey Gilbert and Frobisher, had actually found a way through the ice and thus sailed along a North-west Passage, it was accepted that Franklin's idea of heading south down Peel Sound after leaving Lancaster Sound had taken him to a maze of channels which offered the through route. So today many consider the ill-fated Franklin, whose day-by-day records were discovered by search parties sent out to solve the mystery of his disappearance, to be the actual discoverer of the North-west Passage, for those records proved he knew of the practicable way through the ice.

Thus, misinformed by an inaccurate chart, Sir John Franklin had the instinct of the true explorer, to find and prove the truth of his belief for himself.

Sixty years passed before Roald Amundsen, another explorer lured by the fabulous history of the search for the North-west Passage over the centuries, bought his little craft, which for twenty-seven years had been a fishing-boat in North America, and was of the same age as himself, and prepared it for another onslaught against the ice-screened waterways of the Arctic.

It was a new age, when the fresh lure was the Pole itself, but Amundsen wanted, more than anything else, to bring the long, long search to a successful conclusion.

In 1902 he finally set out across the Atlantic with a crew of seven. He had at one time worked as a waiter in a quayside café to earn money for the journey. He pinned his hopes on two facts. He had read everything he could find about the experiences and discoveries of those who had preceded him, and he had under his feet a craft that drew only six feet of water. He felt the *Gjoa*'s shallow draught gave him an edge over all who had tried to nose through the Arctic waterways in vessels of deeper draught.

In this he was right, for at one time he grounded, and instead of leaving a wreck in the ice he managed to refloat the *Gjoa* and continue to King William Land, where he not only wintered, but stayed for a couple of years. Roald Amundsen, having come this far, had a mind to kill a couple of polar birds with one stone. Besides traversing an open waterway and so completing the voyage through the North-west Passage, he wished to check the position of the North Magnetic Pole. He was able to refix the magnetic pole's position after making a long journey by sledge, and proved that this pole is not a geographical fixture, but has a noticeable degree of movement.

It was August of 1905 when the *Gjoa* left her anchorage in the Arctic and continued the quest for the last stage of the North-west Passage. In Simpson Strait she came within an inch of grounding in several places, but Amundsen nosed his way forward, often holding his breath as he took soundings. Then, on the 26th of the month, he stared with eyes wide open at a stretch of clear water.

The North-west Passage had been made, and Roald Amundsen was the first man to sail across the northern fringe of the vast American land mass.

It was not unfitting that a man of the same historic Viking stock as Bjarni Herjulfson should have crowned with success the efforts and exploits of explorers throughout more than a thousand years of endeavour.

THE FOUNDING OF JOHN COMPANY

T w o events, both in different ways of great historic importance, conspired to empty the pockets of English merchants of cash to provide ships and men for voyages of exploration. One man was vitally concerned in both events.

This was Francis Drake.

He was the first commander of any expedition to circumnavigate the globe. He followed in the track of Magellan, but he roved farther and against greater odds. For whereas Magellan sailed under Spain's flag, Drake was fair prey for any ambitious Spanish or Portuguese sea-captain or island governor with a well-armed galleon at his disposal.

Perhaps if Drake had not had the instincts of a pirate he would never have made his voyage around the world, for he certainly diced for fortune, took great risks, and plundered when he had a mind to – he even kidnapped a navigator when he decided such a course was necessary. But without such rugged individuality, without the readiness to take those often towering risks and the audacity to win through, Drake would never have undertaken his great feat of circumnavigation nor would he have played the part he did in defeating the Spanish Armada eight years after his return from voyaging around the world. For this reason alone it is as well to give the man the Spaniards thought a devil his due.

The voyage round the world took three years. Drake left England in 1577, a veteran mariner who had been engaged in the African slave trade of the day and in removing Spanish property to the holds of English ships in the West Indies and the Caribbean. He had given Elizabeth enough of the loot he had collected to win her approval for a more ambitious project, and once he had the royal sanction he lost no time in fitting out the ships he proposed to take on a voyage to cut the Spanish trade routes.

The ships were five in number, the largest the *Pelican* of a hundred tons and the smallest the *Marigold,* only thirteen tons. His men numbered a hundred and sixty, but they were not told of their commander's intention until the squadron had reached Morocco and there could be no thought of return. On the way he started to collect from the Portuguese, and in one of their vessels he came upon an experienced navigator named Nuno da Silva, whom he offered employment. Da Silva became very friendly with the English commander and was of invaluable service to him.

Possibly da Silva was responsible for Drake wintering in the same harbour on the South American coast chosen by Magellan. Like Magellan, he discovered he had a mutiny on his hands. The ringleader, named Thomas Doughty, was arrested, confessed, and sentenced to death. Drake offered Doughty the alternatives of being marooned, sent back to England to be hanged, or beheaded, and the mutineer chose the last. Drake and Doughty shared a meal together and then went ashore and Doughty put his neck on the block awaiting it and made a joke about his short neck.

When the winter months were over two of the ships were burned. Drake then had the *Pelican,* the *Elizabeth,* and the little *Marigold.* He somehow got all three through the Strait of Magellan and found himself in an ocean he would never have thought of naming Pacific. Almost at once he was battered by a series of terrible gales. The *Elizabeth*'s captain found his ship unmanageable, for it was driven back into the strait they had left, and wisely he kept going rather than risk his craft. When the gales abated it was too late to turn round again, and he continued to England, where he was thrown into prison for deserting his commander.

Before the gales blew themselves out the *Marigold* had vanished under the Pacific waves. Drake decided he might change his luck by changing his ship's name. So the *Pelican* was renamed the *Golden Hind,* a proud name in nautical history, and promptly

He entertained the Sultan aboard the Golden Hind

went cruising after Spanish treasure ships. He stuffed his holds with loot worth more than two million pounds, and then started north to find if his friend Frobisher was right about a seaway across the north of the Americas. He certainly roved as far as Vancouver before he turned around, and he spent a month on the Californian coast before deciding there might be too many Spanish galleons awaiting him in the Atlantic. His best plan seemed to be to continue westward and emulate Sebastian del Cano. So marking California on his chart as New Albion, he formally claimed it for Queen Elizabeth, and then headed for the Moluccas. Reaching Ternate, the capital of the group, he entertained the Sultan aboard the *Golden Hind*, and before sailing on to the Celebes stuffed six tons of cloves on top of the Spanish treasure in his hold. He found some new islands, was nearly wrecked several times, and on one occasion jettisoned three tons of his cloves to lighten his ship, and by the time the Cape of Good Hope was sighted he was down to three barrels of drinking water for fifty-seven men.

The *Golden Hind* was sighted off Plymouth on 3 November 1580. The story of Drake's achievement caught the imagination of his countrymen, as did the vast profit with which he had returned. When the *Golden Hind* sailed to Deptford the Queen came to visit the ship, and the occasion was marked by her knighting its captain and commander.

From that moment English merchants were agog to be trading with the East Indies. In the year of the Armada's defeat, 1588, when their fear of Spanish sea power was largely dissipated, another Englishman, Thomas Cavendish, completed the third circumnavigation of the world through Magellan Strait. It was enough. The way was considered open. A group of London merchants petitioned the Queen for licence to send ships to trade in the East Indies. It was granted, and in 1591 three ships set out, but the craft and their crews were not well chosen, and by the time they had reached the Cape of Good Hope one had to be sent back with the expedition's sick. A second foundered somewhere off the Madagascar coast. Captain Lancaster brought the third ship to the East Indies, but was glad to turn for home. With a gambler's resolve to save something from complete disaster, he headed for the West Indies, which he reached with his ship leaking so badly she had to be beached before she sank under her crew. Not many of her company arrived back in England. They were given a lift in a French privateer.

However, the merchants of London were prepared for setbacks. They belonged to the everyday hazards of such trading, which could produce handsome profits, as Drake and captains of his kidney had amply demonstrated. Moreover, Captain John Lancaster had actually reached the East Indies. Only a few years before that would have been deemed impossible.

So the merchants sent another petition to the Queen, and towards the end of the year 1600 she granted them a trading charter in which they were referred to as the Governor and Company of Merchants of London trading to the East Indies.

That slip of scrolled parchment was the birth certificate of the famous East India Company, to be known by countless of its employees over a great many historic years simply as John Company.

Lancaster, who had certainly shown willing in the service of London's maritime-minded merchants, was commissioned by the new East India Company to take a small fleet of six armed trading ships to procure oriental cargoes. No less than seventy thousand pounds was put up for the venture, enough to provide Lancaster with a vessel of eight hundred tons, the *Red Dragon,* three of three hundred tons, *Ascension, Hector,* and *Susan,* as well as the more modest *Quest* of a hundred tons. John Davis, to be known for his belief in the North-west Passage, was the chief navigator, called in those days the pilot-major. It may be that Davis's arguments in favour of the existence of the northern sea passage he had failed to find helped to win the rival Dutch East India Company's support for Henry Hudson in the attempts to find the passage he made some years later.

On a chilly February day in 1601 Lancaster and his ships sailed down the Thames, laden with goods for export to the value of thirty thousand pounds. The merchant explorers had no mind to start such a venture with any penny-pinching ideas of economy and frugality. They wanted profit, and were prepared to invest to secure it.

It was an attitude that was to prove itself over the next few centuries, and was to evoke an historic sneer from a paunchy little Corsican when he mistakenly labelled the English a nation of shopkeepers. Those shopkeepers had been brought into being by the English explorers who made world-wide trading a veritable craft at which Englishmen came to excel, much to the envy of more martial nations.

Hugging the coast of Brazil, Lancaster found the *Quest* a liability, and he removed her goods and gear and crew and set the sluggish craft adrift. When some of the crew went down with the dreaded scurvy Lancaster produced lemon-juice and insisted his men drink it as an anti-scorbutic. He reached the Cape and anchored for a month, at the end of which time scurvy was no longer a menace. He made several calls on native chiefs before reaching the Moluccas, where he joined forces with some Dutch, who were co-religionists, and in the Malacca Strait a joint Anglo-Dutch operation resulted in the capture of a richly laden galleon.

Lancaster was back in the Thames in 1603, with cargoes so valuable that they choked the London market. That was the year of Elizabeth's death and the arrival of the first Stuart at Westminster. It was also the year Sir Henry Middleton was sent to the Moluccas to establish a permanent English station, and this served as an invitation to other English sea captains to round the Cape of Good Hope and criss-cross the Atlantic, men like that Captain Keeling who not only discovered the islands named after him, but demonstrated that a voyage could be made without any of the crew dying from scurvy.

However, the inevitable happened. Quarrels arose with the Dutch who had also planted themselves in the East Indies, and so the merchants of the East India Company looked around for other sites for trading stations. They settled in India and along the Persian Gulf. Trade prospered, but the Company had a fight on its hands. The Portuguese were not giving up a century-old monopoly easily or with any show of grace. In sea-fights they came off second best, and in time the English wore down resistance after founding factories at Surat and on the Gulf of Cambray in 1612. Eight years later the English captured Ormuz, on the Persian Gulf, and the Portuguese from that time saw their influence in the Indian Ocean wane.

Meantime the French had arrived, as explorers and would-be conquerors, for the sword-in-hand explorer was still very much the fashion in the early seventeenth century. They formed an East India Company in 1604, three years after a certain Pirard da Laval, of St Malo, had in 1601 engaged an English navigator to take him in the steps of da Gama. But the French explorer was lucky to escape with his life when the ship he had acquired broke her back in the Maldives. The sailors rushed to the wine casks when the keel struck rock and were soon too tipsy to trouble whether they were about to join Davy Jones in his notorious locker or live to sail another craft.

When, after some years spent in captivity, de Laval returned to Europe, his enthusiasm for exploration was no longer an urge he could not contain. Referring to the sight of the reeling sailors smelling of wine lees he wrote: 'This filled me with horror, and convinced me that sailors leave their souls and consciences ashore.'

It took the French sixty years to make any impression across the Indian ocean, but by 1664 they had more than a foothold in India and along the Persian Gulf. They also secured Mauritius, and the influence of the French did not fade until Mauritius was captured in 1810, during the struggle with Napoleon. By that time the saga of Robert Clive, the Honourable East India Company's servant in India, had been written into history and the Indian sub-continent had been explored by merchants and military alike.

The Honourable East India Company flourished for the most part during the seventeenth century, and sent its armed representatives to trade and fight as occasion demanded of them. But John Company has to be given the credit for realizing that peaceful penetration could be more lasting than the thrusts of a sword. It sought trading treaties. Indeed, it very early on claimed trading rights from a treaty Francis Drake was said to have signed with the Sultan of Ternate, in the Spice Islands, on the occasion when he acquired his famous six tons of cloves. Because the Dutch concentrated on the Spice Islands and what today is called Indonesia, the English suffered reverses in this part of the East Indies. Indeed, John Company's factor was thrown out of one settlement, and another factor was murdered, and an expedition sent to point out to the Dutch the error of their ways was given no chance to function as ordered because heavy seas stove in ship's timbers and halted Sir Thomas Dale, one-time Governor of Virginia, and his men in their sea-tracks.

That, however, was very much the luck of the game in those years when merchants and mariners could still be described as explorers with a good deal in common.

Later the French made a colonial come-back on Madagascar and in Cochin-China and Indo-China, where French influence remained until after the Second World War. When the British occupied Aden, key point on the Persian Gulf, the French sought an answer and decided they had one when they moved into Djibouti, in Somaliland, but by that time another story of exploration was being written in Africa.

One can say, in effect, that John Company spent the seventeenth century exploring and selecting trading sites and the eighteenth in consolidating what it procured or achieved. But because John Company was served from time to time by brilliant men, both in command of their East Indiamen fleet of distinctive ships with tall hulls and parallel rows of gun-ports, and in charge of their shore establishments, the eighteenth century saw territorial gains that have proved of great significance in modern history.

Such a man was Sir Stamford Raffles.

He was actually born at sea, and became a clerk in the service of John Company at the age of thirteen. He grew to be a man of clear vision. In 1786 the Rajah of Kedah ceded the island of Penang to the East India Company, and this at the time was deemed sufficient to control maritime movement through the Strait of Malacca. After the turn of the century, while Napoleon was still a threat in Europe, the Dutch and the English again came to blows in the East Indies. This time the English did the ousting, and the man who was made Governor of Java was Raffles.

Five years later, after Waterloo, an agreement was signed in Europe between the English and the Dutch by which Java again became Dutch. Raffles was not long out of a job of influence in the East Indies. In 1819 he leased Singapore, a swampy island, from the Sultan of Johore, in the name of the East India Company, and issued a proclamation which stated: ' I have declared that the port of Singapore is a free port and the trade thereof open to ships and vessels of every nation, equally and alike to all.'

A free port and free trade was the logical outcome of the

centuries of struggle and development John Company had undergone, furthering exploration, consolidating colonial development, and evolving an ever-increasing trade overseas that not only made the mother country rich, but helped materially in her becoming a great maritime power.

It has all been summed up in a current catch phrase – the British genius for self-development of colonies. This suggests a glib historical performance which would not have been recognized by the men who did the performing.

John Company through more than two centuries of feverish activity around the world had been compelled to establish its own great fighting fleet and had developed as a mercantile power that even minted its own coins, built forts to protect its stations and factories and ports, and raised its own land armies.

The wars in which it engaged, the efforts it made to stamp out piracy, have no part in the story of famous explorers, but were the logical projections of the desire of other nations to share in the benefits deriving from greater knowledge of the physical world. However, after more than two centuries John Company had served its historic purpose of aiding exploration and consolidating the trade and territorial gains that resulted from such discoveries. In the early nineteenth century Britain was a maritime power with professional seamen manning warships. The bulky, ponderous East Indiamen went out of fashion and so did the famous company owning them. Side by side with the warship was the merchant ship. A new age required new conceptions of trade and protecting trade.

This was apparent before Waterloo decided Europe's future for the next century. In 1814 John Company's Indian monopolies were taken from it, and the trade with India thrown open to all merchants. Nineteen years later, in 1833, its monopoly of the China trade was likewise rescinded. The long ungainly East Indiamen were sold, to sail under other ensigns than the famous St George's Cross on a ground of red and white stripes. The Company's premises were sold, its name removed from ledgers and from over doorways and gateways. Its employees were pensioned off.

Other nations had formed their East India Companies, but it was John Company that endured through the years of struggle

and change. Today there are new nations in the East that can
be said to have their origins in that ferment of trading under
the law that was the Honourable East India Company.

BY WAY OF VENUS

'The mildest-mannered man that ever scuttled ship or cut a throat.' That was Byron's considered opinion of William Dampier, a strange, restless man who has also been described as 'A rolling stone, a man avid for experience, no matter of what kind.'

However shrewd or otherwise those opinions may be, Dampier remains today the epitome of the buccaneer extraordinary, the swashbuckling raider with letters of marque in his doublet who feared no odds and because he lacked fear was curious about men and places, and because he had this inbred curiosity was almost willy-nilly an explorer in his own right. The Dampiers of the world make history despite themselves. They are thrown up by every age which is moving towards vital change.

In his lifetime Dampier was an East Indies trader and a seaman in the navy as well as a ship's captain. He worked on a plantation in the West Indies, became a buccaneer, went roving as a pirate, and also as a privateer. He could make ocean charts, and he sailed round the world twice by Cape Horn in twenty years, was a successful author and for a time the darling of the Royal Society in London. When he died in 1715 the golden age of piracy was dimming fast while his own fame shone brightly, remembered on the maps of the world with a Dampier Archipelago off the north-west coast of Australia and Dampier Land a peninsula on the mainland. Two straits off New Guinea bore his name, one affording mariners the best passage between the Indian and Pacific Oceans.

A man who must have held long conversations with Dampier,

and heard tales told to no other man, was Woodes Rogers, a Bristol-born mariner, recovered from bankruptcy to accept the post of Governor of the Bahamas, where he began clearing the Caribbean of the freebooters infesting it. One of the most notorious pirates run off the high seas by the former privateer was Edward Teach, another Bristol man, who sailed out of New Providence and earned dark fame as the notorious Blackbeard.

However, just what changes were being made in the first half of the eighteenth century can be gauged by a comparison between two captures of Spanish galleons by two men thirty years apart. One was the capture of the Acapulco treasure galleon, *Nuestra Senora de la Encarnacion Desengano,* by Woodes Rogers, who had been told by the knowledgeable Dampier to lie in wait for her at Cape St Lucas, on the California coast. The other was the capture of a similar annual treasure galleon out of Acapulco by Commodore Anson, who circumnavigated the world in his flagship *Centurion.* The second Spanish galleon was being navigated by a Portuguese of considerable reputation, Don Jeronimo de Mentero, who may have known a great deal about tides and currents, but couldn't match the English commodore from Staffordshire in a scrap at sea. Anson's gunners killed sixty-seven of Don Jeronimo's crew and wounded eighty-four before the Spanish colours were pulled down. Anson's losses were two killed and seventeen wounded. In the Spanish galleon's hold were more than one million three hundred thousand pieces of eight and nearly forty thousand ounces of virgin silver.

But there was a difference in status between Woodes Rogers and Anson. The former had been a privateer. The latter was a Royal Navy commander operating in time of war. Anson earned fame as a career admiral who won battles and organized the Royal Marines as a separate entity. He was no explorer. But when he died in 1762 he had made the seas safe for two of the most famous Englishmen of their time, Captain James Cook and Sir Joseph Banks, the men who removed the third word from Terra Australis Incognita.

The great story of the true discovery and settlement of Australia and New Zealand rightfully begins with a young man who never earned as much as a pound a week, and whose career as an explorer was achieved with a telescope that cost half a crown. With that he scanned the heavens at night in the parish of Hoole, near Preston, where he was a sickly curate doomed to die at a very early age.

His name was Jeremiah Horrocks.

As an explorer in his own realm of heavenly exploration he holds a unique place, and it was directly the result of his observations that a voyage was made which took two great men to the Southern Pacific.

It came about in this way. Just before the middle of the seventeenth century the most experienced astronomers in England expected to see the transit of the planet Venus on 6 December 1631. They manned their telescopes only to be disappointed, then went back to their tables of calculations and worked out a sum that informed them the next transit would not occur until a century later. Not unnaturally they lost interest.

Not so young Jeremiah Horrocks with his half-crown telescope. He made some mathematical calculations of his own and decided that the next time Venus passed between the earth and the sun would be in only eight years' time. He told a friend about it, and as a result they were the only two persons in the world to witness the transit of Venus when it occurred on the date Horrocks had correctly calculated, just before sunset on 24 November 1639.

That day was a Sunday, and he hurried from his church duties to man his cheap telescope, with only a bare half-hour to make one of the most important astronomical observations of that era. But in that thirty minutes he successfully measured the distance of the planet Venus from the sun three separate times, and he wrote down the joy he felt.

'Oh, most gratifying spectacle, the object of so many wishes! I perceived a new spot of unusual magnitude, and a perfectly round form, that had just entered upon the left limb of the sun.'

Within a year this brilliant astronomer was dead. But before succumbing to ill-health he had penned a manuscript which he entitled *Venus in Sole Visa*, and purely by chance this came into the possession of a member of the Royal Society after the accession of Charles II. Christian Huygens, the famous Dutch scientist and astronomer, was paying a visit to England at the time and was shown it. He considered it of such importance that he personally sent it to Helvétius, who published it in Danzig in 1662. It is said the Royal Society was responsible for a thorough search for any other papers left by the dead curate, only to learn with dismay that Cromwell's looting Roundheads had broken into his father's house and burned all the bundles of manuscripts they could find. Some which had been sent to a London bookseller had been destroyed in the Great Fire.

More than a century passed after the finding of the manuscript, and a transit of Venus took place exactly as Jeremiah Horrocks had calculated it would. This time astronomers were ready and waiting for it, and it satisfied British scientists that the next transit, in another eight years, should be observed if possible from Tahiti, in the Pacific. Accordingly a vessel was chartered and fitted out to make the journey.

The command was offered to James Cook, who was responsible for the ship chosen being a Whitby collier of 370 tons, the *Earl of Pembroke,* which was renamed *Endeavour.*

At the time he was chosen Cook was virtually unknown in England. He had joined the navy as an able-bodied seaman and had been promoted captain on sheer merit. On merit alone he had been chosen for the voyage to Tahiti to observe the transit of Venus. The astronomer accompanying him was Charles Green. But a second scientist and observer was a young fellow of the Royal Society named Joseph Banks, twenty-five and full of enthusiasm for the chance to undertake scientific exploration. Banks was the son of a well-to-do Lincolnshire family who upon one occasion came out with a retort that has been wryly remembered.

When asked by friends why he did not make the fashionable grand tour of Europe he replied quickly, ' Everyone blockhead does that. My grand tour shall be one round the globe.'

Perhaps the fact that young Banks knew something not known by his friends may have been in part responsible for such confidence. Cook had been issued with instructions from the Admiralty that would send him, after the observation of the transit of Venus, sailing south to latitude forty degrees. If by the time he reached that latitude he had not found Terra Australis he was to proceed east towards that other land sighted by Tasman, which was being called New Zealand by both English and Dutch sea-captains.

The *Endeavour* sailed from England on 25 August 1768,

*The native Maoris, Banks learned, after observing some cleanly
picked bones that were obviously human, were cannibals.*

and eight months later, after an eventful voyage during which Banks had lost his two servants and a landscape artist he had employed, arrived at Tahiti, where the natives welcomed the ship and her company.

Leaving Tahiti, Cook first explored the other islands in the same group and named them the Society Islands after the Royal Society which was responsible for the voyage. Then he sailed south, as instructed, for the indeterminate shore known as New Zealand. Three months dragged by before young Nicholas Young, the boy member of the crew, won the gallon of rum for being the first to sight land. The day was 7 October.

On the 11th began Cook's circumnavigation of the land of New Zealand, which he proved was two large islands. He explored the coastlands, mapped the shores, and organized the foraging parties undertaken by Banks to secure botanical specimens. The native Maoris, Banks learned after observing some cleanly picked bones that were obviously human, were cannibals who ate their enemies killed in battle. Finally, after more than five months in New Zealand waters, Cook made ready to depart westward after unfurling the Union flag on shore and formally claiming New Zealand for the British Crown. On the last day of March 1770 he hoisted sail. On his map he marked the place as Cape Farewell. A short while later New Zealand dropped below the horizon.

Nineteen days later land was again sighted. Through Cook's telescope he saw hills covered with trees and wide stretches of sandy shore. He turned the *Endeavour* and sailed for a further nine days until he saw a bay which offered shelter as a haven. He brought the *Endeavour* inside the headlands and dropped anchor.

A week later the *Endeavour*'s crew pulled up the anchor and Cook sailed on, with a new name on the fresh map he was in process of drawing. It was Botany Bay, suggested by Banks who had enthusiastically rummaged among the incredible number of new plants he had discovered.

When the *Endeavour* arrived in harbour at Batavia in October, and her hull was given a thorough overhaul, her commander received a shock when he saw what the grinding on the Great Barrier Reef had really done to the keel, and how close he had been sailing to disaster during the preceding weeks.

'The keel had been diminished,' Cook said, 'to the thickness of the under-leather of a shoe!'

But the ex-collier from Whitby had held together and remained seaworthy, justifying Cook's belief in her construction, and so the records of the transit of Venus were brought back to England, and with them the records of two new lands of which possession had been taken for the Crown.

It was on 10 July 1771 that Nicholas Young again sighted land. The boy whose first sighting of a New Zealand cape is commemorated on charts by the name Young Nick's Head had now glimpsed the green fields of his native land. Three days later, at three in the afternoon, the *Endeavour*'s crew and passengers landed at Deal, where Julius Caesar had once waded ashore on his own voyage of exploration.

Ten years later the man who has been termed the Father of Australia was created a baronet, and Sir Joseph Banks, an empire-builder both by instinct and inclination, began to canvass the idea of settling the displaced United Empire Loyalists, the real victims of the American Revolutionary War, in New South Wales. One of the Loyalists, James Mario Matra, who had been a midshipman with Cook on that historic first voyage to Australia, visited Banks, and the outcome was a joint appeal to Lord Sydney, who accepted the proposal of colonial development as a solution to a mounting problem. The numbers of convicts in England awaiting transportation to plantations in the West Indies were growing alarmingly. New South Wales offered the prospect for absorbing the Loyalists and the surplus convicts. But when the project was touched upon in the King's speech in 1787 only the convicts were mentioned. The Loyalists had been tacitly omitted. That year the first seven hundred colonists to sail for Botany Bay were accordingly convicts.

In England one man remained who really cared for the new colony. That was Sir Joseph Banks. He was responsible for sending five of the King's famous merino sheep to the colony, thus founding Australia's great pastoral industry.

Cook was in the truest sense a pathfinder. Where he led others could follow. On his second expedition he became the first navigator in history to pass the Antarctic Circle. That was on 17 January 1773. Only the heavy ice encountered by his ship, the *Resolution*, which had lost contact with her consort, the

Adventure, stayed him from continuing farther south than sixty-seven degrees.

On 30 July 1775 the *Resolution* dropped her anchor off Spithead. She had left with a complement of a hundred and twelve officers, scientists, and crew. She returned with a hundred and eight, a truly remarkable feat for that time after a voyage lasting three years and eighteen days. Captain James Cook was for the second time received in private audience by his King as a signal mark of royal favour.

But history was about to intervene in the career of the man who might well lay claim to having been the world's greatest true explorer.

In the spring of 1776 Cook was sent in the *Resolution* to sail round the Cape of Good Hope to Tahiti, where he had always been warmly welcomed, and then to head in a north-easterly direction towards the American mainland, where he was to explore the shores between forty-five and sixty-five degrees North, in the hope of finding a seaway to the Atlantic.

By mid-January, 1778, after a tediously uneventful voyage, Cook sighted some thickly wooded islands with bright flowering trees. He sailed among them and named them the Sandwich Islands after the Earl of Sandwich. Today they are Hawaii.

He went ashore to stop fighting between his men and the natives and was hacked to pieces before anything could be done to save him. James Cook had indeed given his life to the Pacific.

THE CHALLENGE OF AFRICA

FROM the close of the American Revolutionary War the further exploration of the United States could be safely left in the pioneering hands of the new breed of Americans augmented by influxes of Europeans bent on sniffing a different air and often challenging a wilderness. For the most part exploration in the North American continent progressed along national lines, as it did in South America to a very large extent, and later in Australia when the work of Sir Joseph Banks began producing the kind of dividends that make for nationhood.

The same was largely true of the vast land called Russia, which has intrigued and often baffled Western visitors from the time of Chancellor. China remained largely an oriental enigma, and indeed still does, but from the time of the Polos, explorers crossed each other's trails along her deserts and mountains and rivers, and to the Chinese themselves their country was certainly not the geographical enigma it appeared when viewed from either Washington or London.

True, while in southern Cathay, or China, Marco Polo heard tales of the land of Cipango, fifteen hundred miles away, which, he was assured, no traveller had reached. Certainly the navies of the Great Khan had not landed troops to subdue it. In fact this land we know as Japan remained another oriental enigma, despite some later trade with European merchants, especially the Dutch from the East Indies, until a visit from an American ship resulted, in 1859, in the country being opened up for trade with other nations. As long before as the time of Elizabeth I an English ship, the *Charity*, had arrived off the land of cherry blossom and

125

pagodas, and her pilot, a certain William Adams, elected to stay behind when his ship sailed. He married a Japanese woman and taught her countrymen the European methods of shipbuilding. But Bill Adams was more of an energetic lotus-eater than an explorer.

On the other hand, there remained one continent that continued throughout the passing centuries to offer a challenge to explorers of all nations. This was Africa. After its coastline had been navigated it still remained a vast continent with little known of its interior. Many legends had sprung up about the peoples inhabiting it, from Prester John and his kingdom, later to be rationalized as Ethiopia, a Christian land, to the west-flowing branch of the Nile and its strange peoples, later to be rationalized as the Niger, which was no branch of the Nile.

Strangely, it was the continent about which more had been known for longer, because the Nile civilization was among the oldest known and recorded. It was also the continent nearest to most European lands. Yet for a century and a half after da Gama had doubled the Cape of Good Hope at the continent's southern extreme no one thought seriously of settling in a land with a good climate. Chance piled up the wreck of the Dutch ship *Haarlem* near the Cape in 1647, and for twelve months her crew lived under the bulk of Table Mountain. In the following year the Thirty Years' War ended, and the Dutch East India Company sent a rescue party to find out what had happened to the survivors of the *Haarlem*. They found them flourishing and enjoying life, and a couple of them, named Proot and Janssen, gave such an encouraging report on the country that in 1652 Jan van Riebeck was sent back with three ships to found a colony. It was the year William Dampier was born, and ten years after Abel Tasman had sailed from Java to discover Van Diemen's Land.

The founding of that Dutch colony was the first genuine start of opening up Africa, which in the centuries to come was to earn such harsh names as the Dark Continent and the White Man's Grave.

In the years after van Riebeck's coming many men of many races were to accept the challenge of the African continent, and a good many were to surrender their lives in the furtherance of exploration.

One was the Scot, Mungo Park. He was the protégé of Sir Joseph Banks, who between such work as helping to found the Royal Horticultural Society, being President of the Royal Society and Trustee of the British Museum, as well as planning the development of Kew Gardens and establishing similar botanical gardens in Ceylon, St Vincent, and Jamaica, found time to draw up a scheme for the exploration of the tropic regions of Africa. It was the inspiration of Banks that sent Park to Africa as it had sent Flinders and Bass to New South Wales.

Banks founded the African Association in 1788, and one of its objects was to discover the source of the Niger. The first expedition under Houghton failed and the leader was left to die, deserted by his companions. But the second, organized in 1793, was led by the enthusiastic Park, who has often been acclaimed one of the most heroic explorers of all time. His expedition was confronted by almost every conceivable obstacle and hardship, but somehow the enduring Scot survived to reach the Upper Niger, which he explored and to his surprise found flowing from west to east. Mungo Park started out from Gambia in 1796 and reached Segu, but fell sick, and arrived back in Gambia with a slave caravan. When he eventually returned to England to make his report he brought a song which, it has been said, Londoners took to their heart. It had been sung to him by crooning Negresses as he lay shivering with fever in a tent. Park provided the translation :

> ' The wind howled
> And rain poured down.
> The poor white man came
> And sat him down beneath our tree.
> Pity the white man !
> Ye maids and women of the Bambara.
> Alas, he has no mother to bring him milk,
> No wife to grind his corn !'

Mungo Park was lionized by London Society, but he could not settle to an orderly life even when invasion by Napoleon was hourly expected. In the year Nelson laid the bogey of the invasion of Britain for nearly a hundred and forty years, by winning the sea-battle of Trafalgar with the aid of French maritime charts, Park went back to Africa, and shortly after Trafalgar had been fought, in the middle of November 1805, he sent his faithful guide Isaako back to base with most of his private papers.

Isaako also carried a letter Park had written in a moment of prophecy. In it he wrote:

'I intend to make my way to the sea, either via the Congo or some other estuary, and expect to be in Europe again by May or June. Even if all the Europeans who are still with me were to perish, and I myself were half dead, I would persevere. If I do not succeed in reaching my goal I will go to meet my death on the Niger.'

The natives he encountered became hostile. A large raft was constructed. Mungo Park launched himself upon the river always associated with his name. But no further word came from him. In January 1810 the Governor of Sierra Leone dispatched the guide Isaako to find out if he could procure news of the lost expedition. Eight months later, in Sansanding, he came upon the man who had been Park's interpreter, Amadi Fatuma, who upon recognizing Isaako is said to have broken down and wept.

'They are all dead!' he exclaimed over and over.

According to the story he told the guide, there had been trouble with the natives at the swift-flowing Bussa rapids, and Park had been forced to open fire. But the white men had been overwhelmed, and the last Fatuma saw of the expedition's leader was when Park grabbed hold of another white man and leaped with him into the foaming rapids. The two locked-together bodies had been swept away like corks.

Sixteen years later Hugh Clapperton, who had been a schooner skipper on Lake Erie and was another Scot, was able with Dixon Denham, a Londoner, to reach Bussa and discover that a legend existed among the natives about the white man who had floated down the river. Clapperton had gone in search of a German explorer, Friedrich Konrad Hornemann, who had also sought the Niger's source, and like Park had dreamed of finding Timbuktu of persistent legend.

Hornemann vanished, another victim of the fatal lure of Africa. Clapperton himself was to succumb to this deadly enchantment. Both he and Denham returned to Africa, Denham to die of fever in Sierra Leone, Clapperton to press on with his companion Richard Lander to explore the Niger's lower reaches.

They reached Sokoto, where Clapperton died on 13 April 1827 of fever. Lander came back with the dead explorer's diaries, but with his brother John started out again to explore the Dark Continent in 1830. Somewhere among the mouths of the Niger he was captured by slavers and was not liberated until a Liverpool merchant was able to secure his release. But he was a restless man and found trouble easily. In February 1834 he died of a wound caused by a poisoned arrow and was buried in the Cameroons.

In the first half of the nineteenth century the White Man's Grave was certainly earning its name.

The man who found Timbuktu and returned to describe it was the Frenchman René Caillié, who was only seventeen when he joined Gray's expedition in 1816 to try to find the vanished Mungo Park. Caillié could no more help being an explorer than he could help breathing. He wrote:

' As soon as I could read and write I was taught a trade. I quickly grew tired of it and spent all my time reading books of travel. I borrowed geographical works and maps. The map of Africa, on which I could see nothing but blank areas, described as unexplored, excited my fantasy more than all the others. This hobby grew into a passion, for the sake of which I gladly renounced everything else.'

One of the works he had read was Mungo Park's *Travels in the Interior of Africa,* which had been published in 1799, when the Negresses' song was being hummed in London salons. Ten years after joining Gray's expedition he had saved enough money to fit out his own caravan and attempt to win an award of two thousand francs offered by the Paris Geographical Society to the first French explorer to bring back proof that he had found Timbuktu.

Caillié set out from Kakondy, in Sierra Leone, where the British liked him, in April 1827. His plodding journey became a terrible ordeal, for the route he chose was along the Upper Niger, where Park had explored, and then over the hard country of the Futa Jalon range. There was a period of days when he merely lay where he fell, expecting to die, unable to rise because of a terrible pain which gripped him. When the pain passed, leaving him very weak, he forced himself to struggle on, and it was almost a year after setting out that, on 20 April 1828, he reached Timbuktu, to learn with terrible bitterness that he was not the first, but the second, white man to reach the city of legend. The first had been Alexander Gordon Laing, a determined Scot who had arrived almost two years before.

Caillié, however, earned his reward as the first Frenchman, but when he returned to Europe he had a sad tale to tell. Laing had been murdered by the Tuaregs as a Christian dog almost as soon as he arrived at Timbuktu. He had been called a spy. Caillié undoubtedly saved his own life by posing as an Egyptian. He was shown the place where Laing had died by some of the Scotsman's murderers. When, almost dead on his feet, he at length arrived in Tangier he had covered three thousand miles on an expedition lasting five hundred and thirty-eight days, a good many of them a living nightmare of terror and pain. The French consul reported to his superiors in Paris :

> ' Caillié is the victor of Timbuktu. He has crossed Africa as a
> beggar. In this condition he threw himself upon the hospi-
> tality of my house. I took him in, and deemed myself fortunate
> indeed that I was the first Frenchman to embrace him.'

René Caillié was fêted in France, given a pension of six thousand francs and made a knight of the Legion of Honour. The son of a baker's assistant in a village of Poitou had come a very long way, but almost every kilometre had been a tough one. That was the only gaurantee Africa gave the explorers bold enough to launch themselves into the continent's interior.

It was yet another Scot who made perhaps the greatest impact on the world as an African explorer. This was David Livingstone.

It was in 1841 that he joined the missionaries then in Bechuanaland, and immediately felt the lure that was Africa's own enchantment. Like Caillié, he had arrived the hard way. At the age of ten he was working in a cotton mill in Blantyre, not far from Glasgow, from six in the morning until eight at night for a few shillings a week. Just as Caillié read every book on geography he could come by, so Livingstone studied Latin in bed at night by the light of a farthing candle. Latin was important for he was determined to become a doctor. He also

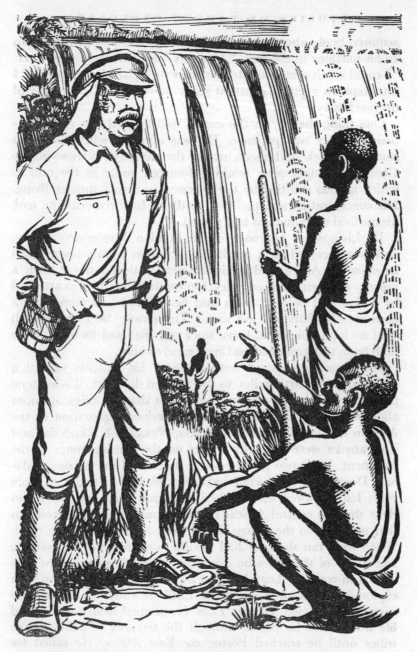

. . . explore the Zambesi eastwards until he came to the mighty cascade he named Victoria Falls

acquired books about history and science, and propped them up on his machine in the mill. ' This way,' he said many years later, ' I could catch sentence after sentence as I passed at my work. I thus kept up a pretty constant study undisturbed by the roar of the machinery.'

One thing the boy in the cotton mill learned was concentration. Another was patience. He was nineteen when he began studying Greek and medicine in the evenings, journeying to Glasgow at night after working fourteen hours in the mill to which he was still tied by the necessity to earn a meagre living. His concentration and patience paid off. In three years he took his medical examinations and passed.

Dr Livingstone approached the London Missionary Society, and was accepted as a missionary. He was twenty-seven when he sailed for Africa, and in his first year in the continent made a journey of seven hundred miles. On one occasion he was attacked by a lion and he afterwards said he suffered ' no more than a permanently damaged left arm.' The pawky Scot thenceforth held no high opinion of lions, since one that had its teeth in his flesh hadn't succeeded in making a meal of him.

His reputation spread until some of his patients walked a hundred and thirty miles to be treated by him. Livingstone planned to undertake wider explorations than his original duties allowed, and at the time he started serious exploration of the African interior Kenya and Uganda, Nyasaland, Rhodesia, and Tanganyika were all blank spaces on the existing maps of the continent. With two white hunters he crossed the blazing Kalahari Desert and discovered Lake Ngami, and within two more years had explored the Zambesi and found that its course ran right through central Africa. He began an ambitious expedition that took him to the Congo. From there he set out for the coast. When food ran short he had trouble with some of his natives, and many of the tribes he came upon were hostile, but he succeeded in reaching Loanda. After a rest he started back and then explored the Zambesi eastwards until he came to the mighty cascades he named Victoria Falls. He seemed to live a charmed life indeed, for he passed through the territory of other hostile tribes until he reached Portuguese East Africa. He sailed for Britain, where he arrived some sixteen years after leaving for Africa, to find himself famous.

In London he shook hands with another famous African explorer, Dr Heinrich Barth, of Hamburg. Barth had returned from Africa in the previous year, the one survivor of an expedition to the north of the continent sponsored by the British. Over a period of five and a half years he had won fame for his penetration and exploring of the vast Sahara and for traversing the Sudan in a gruelling expedition that covered more than ten thousand miles.

The two great explorers held clasped hands for a long time, both feeling the emotional tug of such a meeting, for they were men who had several times been presumed lost as so many other African explorers had been. Between them, Barth the German in the north, Livingstone the Briton in the south, had laid wide the main gateways to the continent's interior, and had demonstrated that the African challenge could be successfully accepted.

Barth did not return to Africa, but already on his journeyings he had experienced a meeting that was to be paralleled in Livingstone's later career as African explorer. He had spent seven months in Timbuktu, often fearful for his life. Indeed, he was probably able to return from Africa for no other reason than the fear the Arabs had of his new Colt revolver. It proved as devastatingly convincing to them as it did to the redman of the American West. Finally, on 18 May 1854, he received the necessary permission from Sheikh El Bakcy to leave Timbuktu. When he reached a region where he was known it was to learn his obituary had been published in German newspapers and an expedition led by a Dr Edward Vogel was on its way to try to find trace of another lost explorer.

It seems incredible, but the two explorers, Vogel and Barth, actually ran into each other. Here is how Barth related the meeting:

' I was riding three miles in advance of the caravan, accompanied only by my faithful servant Mohammed, when I saw a person of most strange appearance approaching – a young man with a snow-white skin, which after these many years seemed to me to be a sign of sickness. I saw that one of his black companions – it was a former servant of mine called Madi – suddenly rushed up to the young man and shouted a few words to him. Then the white man, who was none other

133

than Dr Vogel himself, who had been sent out to search for me, spurred his horse and galloped towards me. Our astonishment at this chance meeting can well be imagined; neither of us had even suspected that we might meet here in the jungle.'

The famous meeting between Livingstone and Stanley is of course more widely known. It took place after Livingstone had returned to Africa as British Consul in Quelemane and with a sum of five thousand pounds to cover the cost of an expedition to explore the Zambesi valley. He left England in 1858, began exploring the Zambesi in a steam launch, the *Ma-Robert*, and along the Shire River came to the great sheet of water that is Lake Nyasa. He explored the entire area by boat and on foot. He returned to report that he wished to continue his explorations alone, and so in 1865 set out again, and, leaving the southern shore of Lake Nyasa, he started the most impressive journey of his life, one lasting in all eight years, during which time he discovered the lakes Mweru and Bangweulu as well as exploring and making a map of Lake Tanganyika. He hoped to find the Nile's source, but before he could accomplish this his health broke down, natives ran off with his medicines, and he made for Ujiji.

Meanwhile in both Europe and America anxiety for the intrepid explorer's safety was growing. There had been no report from him for a long while, and when Livingstone's bearers, who had deserted and left him with mounds of baggage, reached the coast they lied to protect themselves. They claimed their master had fallen into the hands of the cruel Mazitu. Henry Morton Stanley, who wrote for James Gordon Bennett's *New York Herald*, had little persuading to do to get his employer to agree to his arranging an expedition and going to Africa in search of Livingstone. Bennett himself was a red-haired Scot who had emigrated to the United States after being a pedlar in the streets of Glasgow. He had crossed the Atlantic to make a very sizeable fortune when Livingstone was only six.

He gave his best-paid journalist implicit instructions when they met in the Grand Hotel in Paris.

' Draw a thousand pounds now,' he said, ' and when you have gone through that draw another thousand, and when that is spent draw another thousand, and when you have finished that draw another thousand, and so on. But find Livingstone!'

Stanley left at the beginning of October 1870. Exactly a year later Livingstone returned to Ujiji, and a month later the famous meeting occurred. Livingstone wrote:

'When my spirits were at their lowest ebb the Good Samaritan was close at hand. The American flag at the head of a caravan told me the nationality of the stranger. Bales of goods, baths of tin, huge kettles, cooking-pots, tents, etc., made me think, "This must be a luxurious traveller, and not one at his wits' end like me".'

Stanley, however, had been born in Denbigh, in a workhouse, the son of a grazier named John Rowland. He sailed to New Orleans as a cabin boy and was adopted by a cotton broker named Stanley. No one could have had a more romantic career. His own description of the meeting with Livingstone has been familiar to every generation for almost a century. He wrote of it:

'I came in front of the semicircle of Arabs, in the front of which stood the white man with the grey beard. As I advanced towards him I noticed he was pale, looked wearied, had a grey beard, wore a bluish cap with a faded gold band round it, had on a red-sleeved waistcoat, and a pair of grey tweed trousers. I would have run to him, only I was a coward in the presence of such a mob – would have embraced him, only, he being an Englishman, I did not know how he would receive me; so I did what cowardice and false pride suggested was the best thing – walked deliberately to him, took off my hat, and said:
"Dr Livingstone, I presume?"
"Yes," he said, with a kind smile, lifting his cap slightly.'

Stanley wasn't invariably accurate, as his calling Livingstone an Englishman reveals, but by the time of the meeting Africa had cast its spell on him. Stanley the American journalist became Sir Henry Stanley, a notable African explorer who continued Livingstone's exploring work after the latter's death in 1873.

His claim to fame as an explorer lies chiefly in his determined exploring of the Congo as far as the sea and also his solving the riddle of the Nile's source, by proving that the White Nile has actually two sources, Lake Victoria, and also Lake Albert with a small secondary sheet of water, Lake Edward. In short, Stanley completed and set his seal on work done years before by Richard Burton and John Speke, who had been sent from England by the Royal Geographical Society to find the White Nile's source. Speke, almost blind and going deaf, had discovered Lake Victoria after Burton had gone sick. Information he later gave another explorer named Samuel Baker enabled the other man to discover Lake Albert.

When Stanley left Africa in the eighties, to return to England and become a Member of Parliament, a great deal of light had been shed in the dimmest corners of the Dark Continent. The high wave of European colonizing was rolling towards its many shores, and Africa was no longer the grim and enigmatic land of challenge it had been since the days of Ptolemy.

TO THE POLES

FROM 1606, when Captain John Smith arrived in Virginia, the major thrust of North American exploration was very naturally northward, but also westward. Smith explored north and named the land New England, although Cape Cod had been discovered back in 1602 by Bartholomew Gosnold. When the Pilgrim Fathers landed from the *Mayflower* in 1620 and settled territory that became the Commonwealth of Massachusetts domestic exploration of North America by settlers and colonists was given both impetus and purpose. Spaniards and French explored the south and west areas, but from Maine to Georgia the colonists of British stock started thrusting westward, and when Daniel Boone reached Kentucky in 1776 it was to demonstrate the kind of leap forward the new race of pioneers could achieve.

In Canada, Champlain explored to the Great Lakes in 1615 and grew ambitious to continue to the Pacific, but it was not till 1681 that René La Salle explored the Mississippi to the Gulf of Mexico and claimed the land there for France, naming it Louisiana after the French King. It was because of this French cordon from Quebec and Montreal in the north to New Orleans in the south that the British felt compelled to take measures that were deemed precautionary, for war between British and French in North America seemed inevitable. One of those measures was sending George Vancouver, one of Captain Cook's officers, to explore the west coast of North America, with instructions to find that elusive North-west Passage if he could. But by that time history had caught up with the planners. Canada was British, the United States had been declared independent of the British

Crown, and the later Louisiana Purchase was to dictate the shape history and exploration were to take south of the Canadian border, with Meriwether Lewis and William Clark leaping across the Rockies and discovering territory that became the States of Oregon and Washington. Behind the explorers followed the mountain men and scouts to consolidate the territorial gains.

North of the Canadian border the Hudson Bay Company did its own exploring. As a result Samuel Hearne set out to find rumoured copper-mines and discovered the Coppermine River, which he explored into the Arctic as early as 1769, and on his return stumbled upon the Great Slave Lake. Twenty years later Alexander Mackenzie followed a west-flowing river from that lake to what he thought was the Pacific. He too arrived in the Arctic. He later went down the Fraser River, only to find it became unnavigable, and the delay meant that when he reached the Pacific he was too late to meet Vancouver's expedition. But Canada had been crossed, and for neighbours it had not only the newly created United States, but the looming Arctic, with somewhere in its icy fastness the North Pole.

James Gordon Bennett, the imaginative Scots-American from Glasgow's streets who sent Stanley to find Livingstone, was the father of the man responsible, a few years later, for starting a new fashion in exploration – to reach the North Pole. He too was named James Gordon Bennett. He saw an Arctic expedition sponsored by his paper, the *New York Herald,* as a means of creating widespread public interest and thereby increasing the *Herald's* circulation. The idea did not actually originate with him, but he was quick to see the possibilities when it was put to him by Lieutenant Commander George Washington De Long of the US Navy.

Backed by Bennett's cash and enthusiasm, the young naval officer set about acquiring a three-masted barque, the *Jeannette,* and picking a crew for her. She was fitted with an auxiliary steam engine, and was sailed around the Horn to Mare Island in California. Naval experts had doubts about her capacity to perform the task that would be demanded of her, but Bennett could not brook delay, so De Long continued with his original plan.

He reached St Michael, in Alaska, and mistakenly engaged a couple of local Indians instead of Eskimos as hunters and drivers for his dog teams, and sailed on, to freeze fast in the ice just past Bering Strait on 6 September 1879. He was actually at Wrangel Island, but when he set to work exploring the locality he found another small island which he named Herald Island, in recognition of Bennett's aid. The next summer did not bring the expected advance, and when the Arctic winter returned the *Jeannette* was again quickly icebound and the expedition held up until late spring. By the summer of 1881 De Long's coal supply was getting down. He decided to use only sail, but the Arctic had a different idea. The ice holding the ship, far from breaking up, packed in more tightly, and at last penetrated the *Jeannette*'s crushed ribs of timber.

The barque was doomed.

The nearest point on the mainland was Lena Delta, five hundred miles distant. Thirty-three men left their spare clothing and personal belongings behind, taking only the lost ship's log, papers, and scientific data as well as essential supplies for the journey. The night before they started a grim trek over the ice the ship they had abandoned, crushed like a toy, slid out of sight. They were actually on a drifting floe, which carried them twenty-five miles farther north before swinging south. They named land they saw Bennett Island before reaching the largest of the New Siberian group. The party split into three. Only one section reached the mainland. It was not De Long's.

The next spring the bodies of De Long and the eleven men who had been in his party were found frozen in the great white wasteland. Close to De Long's was his diary. The final words he had written were: 'October 30th, Sunday, hundred and fortieth day, Boyd and Goertz died during night, Mr Collins dying.'

There was a curious sequel.

Three years after De Long's death some of the *Jeannette*'s stores were collected by an Eskimo from West Greenland who was seal-hunting. Those forgotten and lost supplies paid for by James Gordon Bennett had drifted over the roof of the world.

When Fridtjof Nansen, a young Norwegian, read of this unplanned voyage of the *Jeannette*'s stores he believed he had discovered a way to reach the North Pole. He was twenty-three. At that time ski-ing was an entirely Norwegian sport when it was not merely a means of crossing snow on foot because no other way was possible. In 1888 he crossed the Greenland icecap on skis and returned with plans for an Arctic expedition which was quite revolutionary. He would take a ship into the ice-floes at a point where Arctic currents would drift it over the top of the world, perhaps very close to the Pole itself.

The ship he had specially built was the *Fram,* which left Oslo, then named Christiania, on Midsummer's Day 1893. On 22 September the *Fram* was secured to a floe, and Nansen awaited the coming of winter. When the ice squeezed her hull the ribs did not crack. Because of her special design she was squeezed upward and out of the ice pincers, to remain safe on the drifting floe.

The *Fram,* in short, was drifting like the *Jeannette's* stores. Moreover, she was actually moving towards the Pole.

However, after nearly eighteen months of patient waiting Nansen realized something only experience could make clear. Progress was too slow for his supply of stores, and he knew the current was not entirely predictable. The *Fram* would pass farther from the Pole than he had supposed.

He and another companion decided to make a dash for the Pole. On 14 April 1895, Fridtjof Nansen and Hjalmar Johansen reached eighty-six degrees fourteen minutes north, the highest latitude any man had ever reached, before they had to turn back. They reached Franz Josef Land and took ship to Norway. The *Fram* also returned after being held in the Arctic ice for thirty-five months.

Nansen's great exploit, although it failed in its objective, served to inspire the great Roald Amundsen to think of reaching the North Pole. But first there was the North-west Passage. If he could find that long-sought seaway he would obtain all the backing he required for an expedition to find the North Pole. So in 1905 he sailed the *Gjoa* and found the North-west Passage, and upon his return was offered enough financial aid to prepare for the polar dash. He was making his preparations when he heard that a friend of his, a ship's doctor named Frederick A. Cook, with whom he had sailed in a Belgian Antarctic exploration ship, the *Belgica,* had reached the Pole.

Amundsen stroked his bushy moustache and smiled shyly. He was pleased for his friend, sorry for himself.

Hard on the heels of this news came word that an American,

Robert Edwin Peary, had reached the Pole and had furthermore called Cook an impostor and a liar.

Peary, as forthcoming proof showed, was telling the truth. Cook was completely discredited.

The American was a man who had carefully planned a polar attempt by sledge. He was a veteran of the Arctic, having made his first journey inside the Arctic Circle in 1885. Like De Long, Peary was a US Navy officer. When serving in the Caribbean he felt that the achievement of Columbus might be matched by a man of modern times reaching the North Pole. From that moment he lived for one thing – to reach the North Pole.

His expedition into Greenland in 1891 was in the nature of a training excursion. Even with a broken leg he carried on to be the first man to arrive at northern Greenland, with his companion Eivind Astrup. Moreover, Peary had gone by sledge. He made several similar expeditions, and on one found three large meteorites, which he brought back to the United States.

In 1908 he felt ready for the big attempt. He sailed in the *Roosevelt*, commanded by Captain Bob Bartlett, to the north of Ellesmere Island, where the winter was spent until mid-February, when Peary started out to make his first supply camp. By 1 March 1909 the final preparations were being made, and on the 30th Peary, with his Negro servant Matthew Henson, and two Eskimos, started out from the advance camp called Cape Columbia. They had two dog teams. At the end of a week those huskies were panting, the first dogs to reach the North Pole. Peary started to build a cairn of stones on the exact location of the North Pole, and over this he raised the American flag.

When he reached civilization again he told his news and wired a laconic message : ' Stars and Stripes nailed to the Pole.'

This was the news that started Roald Amundsen thinking of preparing an expedition to the South Pole, still to be reached.

As a matter of fact, there had been no comparable interest centred on the South Pole by explorers in the southern half of the American continent, as there had been on the North Pole by United States citizens.

True, the great scientific explorer Alexander von Humboldt had traversed the Andes and penetrated deep into the watersheds of the Amazon and the Orinoco, and his efforts in the north of

South America were to a large extent continued farther south by Charles Darwin when he arrived some years later in the *Beagle*. It was on this notable voyage of exploration which became a circumnavigation of the world that Darwin thought out the essential arguments supporting a new theory, one he called evolution and outlined in his *Origin of Species*. Since Darwin's time there have been intermittent attempts to penetrate the dense jungles of the South American interior, and although explorers have given their lives in more recent generations, just as Orellana the Conquistadore did in 1545, trying to penetrate what is still largely a mystery, there remain large tracts of the southern continent's interior, like the Mato Grosso, that jealously retain whatever secrets they hold.

Forty years ago, in 1925, Colonel Percy Harrison Fawcett led an expedition into this unknown region. One object of his journey was to prove the truth or otherwise of a persistent rumour that had existed for centuries about a lost race that lived in what was virtually a lost land. Neither Fawcett nor his companions returned. A rescue expedition was led in search of them, but no trace was discovered, and their fate remains unknown.

Thirteen years before Fawcett's party took off into the Brazilian jungle the South Pole was reached – twice.

It is very possible that at the beginning of this century American whalers and seal hunters might have discovered some Antarctic islands not named on printed maps, but they were men jealous of what they considered their preserves and had no intention of encouraging newcomers who might be, in their eyes, little better than poachers. Graham Land was claimed by both the United States and Britain, and the British sealer James Weddell had announced his finding of an area he named George IV Sea, but which is today marked more appropriately on maps Weddell Sea. This was an area where hard contrary winds blew and progress of any kind was an exhausting task. After Charles Wilkes, yet another US Navy officer, had returned from discovering Wilkes Land, James Ross went into the Antarctic with the *Erebus* and *Terror* and named a couple of volcanoes after his ships, but it was not until 1874 that the British steamship *Challenger* crossed the Antarctic Circle on a research mission. She was the first.

Nineteen years later a Norwegian, Carl Anton Larsen, led

a landing party into Antarctica, and a member of it was Cartson Egeberg Borchgrevink, an explorer of mixed parentage, British and Norwegian. He it was who was the leader of another expedition that spent an entire winter in the Antarctic. After that the new breed of polar explorers readied themselves for what had to come, the onslaught on the South Pole.

One of the first to be attracted to the possibility of reaching the southern Pole was Robert Falcon Scott. He took the *Discovery*, a ship specially designed for the work, to the south polar regions in 1901, and with her a ballon for surveying regions considered inaccessible. Two Antarctic years were spent in the ice of the Ross Sea. In the company of Ernest Shackleton and Edward Wilson, Scott made a journey by sledge that brought the three explorers within eight degrees of the South Pole. They were turned back by a crushing blizzard, by the onset of an attack of scurvy, and by the sudden shortage of food, James Ross's Mount Erebus was their landscape guide on that gruelling return journey.

Scott went back to the land that was eventually to be his grave and performed much valuable research work in the following year. Shackleton, who had been laid low by that journey of nine hundred and fifty miles under bad conditions, returned to the White South in 1907. He came in the *Nimrod,* with gear for more scientific research. He climbed Mount Erebus and located the South Magnetic Pole, and in the following year, setting out in October with three companions, he tried to reach the South Pole with sledges drawn by Manchurian ponies. The ponies proved a bad choice of locomotive power, and although they arrived within two degrees of the Pole they couldn't go on, and were fortunate to get back to the *Nimrod* before the ice imprisoned her for another winter.

They had left the Union Jack flying less than a hundred and fifty miles from the South Pole.

Within a few months the Stars and Stripes were flying from Peary's cairn over the North Pole.

The polar regions were bright with bunting that winter and spring of 1908-1909, all of it red, white and blue.

Less than two years later Scott was back in the Antarctic with a new ship, the *Terra Nova.* In January 1911 he was making various scientific observations preparatory to launching a fresh attempt to reach the Pole in the coming November. He was not to know it, but Roald Amundsen, disappointed from being first to reach the North Pole by Peary's feat, had resolved to be first to reach the South Pole, and actually made his first bid in the September, while Scott waited at McMurdo Sound. He called his camp Cape Evans. Amundsen's base was Whale Bay, sixty miles nearer to the Pole.

Amundsen, who had come south in Nansen's polar ship, the *Fram*, was putting his trust in sledges pulled by huskies, as Peary had. Scott had decided to repeat Shackleton's experiment with ponies.

On the September dash Amundsen was unlucky. Some of his companions suffered severely from frost-bite, and he felt compelled to return. By mid-October the temperature was a number of degrees higher and the winds less fierce. The second attempt began on 20 October. However, they ran into a blizzard, and had to mark their trail for the eventual return journey with markers made of dried fish. They reached Shackleton's southerly limit and in triumph hoisted the Norwegian flag on the leading sledge. A week later they were at the Pole, on 14 December, over which they erected a tent above which flew the flag taken from the leading sledge.

Scott's attempt to reach the Pole began on 24 October, four days after Amundsen's second had been started. On the last day of 1911 they were still two degrees from their objective. By that time the attendant parties had turned back. Scott's own polar party remained for the final dash. The party comprised five, Scott himself, Captain Oates, Lieutenant Bowers, Petty Officer Evans, and Dr Wilson. It was Bowers whose keen sight first caught the colour of the Norwegian flag against the surrounding whiteness.

When they reached the Norwegians' tent they found inside a letter from Amundsen to Scott. In it the winner in what had become a race to the South Pole requested Scott to forward a letter addressed to the King of Norway in the event of Amundsen not surviving the trip back to Whale Bay.

It was a grim piece of irony of the kind that runs like a thread through the history of exploration. For Scott was the one who did not survive. Nor did any member of his polar party. In fact, it is the pathos of Scott's return from the South Pole to a cruel

The second attempt began on 20 October

death that makes the epic one of the most poignant in the history of world exploration.

They had covered two-thirds of the return when the temperature dropped to minus forty degrees Fahrenheit, and they were overwhelmed by unexpected blizzards. In his diary Scott wrote: 'Amongst ourselves we are unendingly cheerful, but what each man feels in his heart I can only guess.' Petty Officer Evans had succumbed and died on 17 February.

A month later, on 16 March, they were a hundred and twenty miles from Cape Evans, and Oates was almost crippled with frost-bite. While a fresh blizzard howled outside their flimsy tent Oates forced himself to stand and said as nonchalantly as he could, 'I'm just going outside, and may be some time.'

He opened the tent flap. When it dropped he vanished into a thick curtain of snow, a gallant man going to his death to remove the burden of himself from the other three.

Scott wrote of him: 'It was the act of a brave man and an English gentleman. We all hope to meet the end with a similar spirit, and assuredly the end is not far.'

The weary trio, Scott, Bowers and Dr Wilson, kept going until 20 March. That night they camped a bare eleven miles from one of their supply points, One Ton Depot, where they would find the supplies they so desperately needed. But next day yet another blizzard made the slow trudge onward impossible. That blizzard lasted nine days and nights. The last entry made in Scott's diary was dated 29 March. It read:

'I do not think we can hope for any better things now. We shall stick it out to the end, but we are getting weaker, of course, and the end cannot be far. It seems a pity, but I do not think I can write any more. R. Scott.'

Beneath this was a line he had forced himself to pen with his last strength: 'For God's sake look after our people.' Like Oates, his last thoughts had not been for himself.

The three bodies in their sleeping bags were not found until that harsh winter had blown itself out. A cross was erected on the site. Carved into it were Tennyson's words: 'To strive, to seek, to find, and not to yield.'

In the year after Colonel Fawcett vanished in the Mato Grosso, Roald Amundsen reached the North Pole, in an Italian airship with General Umberto Nobile and the American Lincoln Ellsworth, who had first flown with Amundsen across the polar regions in the previous year, but had missed flying over the North Pole.

Later the Italian general tried to fly over the North Pole again, without Amundsen, but he crashed, and he and his survivors were stranded in a pitiless wilderness. Amundsen arranged to fly out to rescue them. On 18 June 1928 he took off from Tromsoe in an aircraft piloted by Leif Dietrichsen – and vanished.

Another touch of irony, for in their last resting-places Scott and Amundsen, who both reached the South Pole, remain literally Poles apart, claimed by the eternal snows they had challenged, even in unintentional rivalry with each other.

It is a tribute to the polar pioneers that today, nearly half a century after Amundsen disappeared on an early polar flight, aircraft on regular commercial flights criss-cross the North Pole as a matter of routine, while in the Antarctic those rival Powers that emerged after the Second World War to dominate the Jet Age, the Soviet Union and the United States, have constructed their scientific base camps in the furtherance of securing knowledge about the Frozen South.

In these days bright bunting flies regularly in the polar winds, but only because men prepared to give their lives had the hardihood to accept a great challenge and the faith in themselves to carry through to success or death or, upon occasion, both.

OUT OF THIS WORLD

M E N have not only been attracted to explore the surface of the world in which they live. They have also explored its depths and its heights. The nineteenth century in Europe saw the beginning of what became a sport for the hardy and fit, mountaineering, often a test of nerve and endurance that ended in disaster as well as triumph, as was the case in the epic conquest of the alpine peak the Matterhorn, by Edward Whymper and his party in 1865. One by one the great peaks of the earth's mountain ranges have been scaled, until in 1953 the British Everest Expedition, led by Sir John Hunt, made a formidable attack on the highest, Everest, which was finally surmounted by a Union Jack after a Sherpa named Tenzing and a New Zealander named Edmund Hillary had reached that summit which for so long had denied itself to other intrepid mountaineers.

Alongside the Union Jack they placed the flags of India and of the United Nations.

The new age had new allegiances, as well as new flags.

Explorers of the ocean's depths began later because quite obviously they needed the right kind of equipment, which had to be invented by scientists with an understanding of the particular requirements of what has come to be known as oceanography. But the real advance was made when in the summer of 1934 the American scientist and underwater explorer William Beebe let himself be lowered to a depth of more than three thousand feet in a cylinder called a bathysphere. This was off Bermuda. From the confines of his bathysphere he was able to explore, for the first time, the ocean bed at such a depth.

Afterwards he wrote his experiences in a book entitled *Half Mile Down*.

Fifteen years later another American, Otis Barton, descended off California to a depth of four thousand five hundred feet.

Five years afterwards, in February 1954, two Frenchmen, Georges Houot and Pierre-Henri Willm, descended off the coast of West Africa to a depth of more than thirteen thousand feet, in a bathysphere specially constructed by French naval engineers to plans and specifications drawn up by Professor Auguste Piccard.

After exploring the depths and the heights there remained only the space surrounding the globe that is man's home.

It is symptomatic of the speed with which technical advances are made in the second half of the twentieth century that three years after Houot and Willm dropped two and a half miles to a distant seabed, and four years after Everest was climbed for the first time, by Tenzing and Hillary, an International Geophysical Year was proclaimed. Not only were bases set up in the Antarctic, which was crossed from coast to coast, but the US submarine *Nautilus,* after a couple of exploratory runs, actually 'pierced' the North Pole at a little more than the depth Houot and Willm had dropped off West Africa. This momentous event occurred at eleven-fifteen on the evening of 3 August 1958. The commander of the *Nautilus,* William R. Anderson, and his men stood silent in prayer as their craft actually crossed the pole.

Like the *Nautilus,* the *Skate,* another US nuclear-powered submarine, made underseas voyages to and from the Pole to demonstrate the practicability of polar travel under the ice floes. A less practicable attempt with a submarine had been made more than a quarter of a century before by the British explorer Sir Hubert Wilkins with another submarine named *Nautilus* as a tribute to the fancy of Jules Verne. He had tried to drill his way through blocked passages, but had been forced to desist.

While Anderson and the *Nautilus* were adding their quota of achievement to the International Geophysical Year the scientists of the Soviet Union prepared their own spectacular demonstration. On 4 October they launched Sputnik 1, an artificial earth satellite not quite two feet in diameter which rose from its launching site and started travelling in an ellipse varying in distance from the earth between five hundred and a hundred and twelve miles. Sputnik I was a groping into space that lasted for three months.

It was spun into the atmosphere like a coin on 4 October 1957, and a month later Sputnik II followed, six times the weight of the first, and spinning nine hundred miles away from the earth's gravitational pull to exist as a satellite for an historic one hundred and sixty-one days. Sputnik II actually carried a passenger, a lively, bright-eyed dog named Laika, fitted with apparatus for supplying her with food and air and recording her temperature and heart beats. There was also the means of providing Laika with instantaneous death when Sputnik II stopped being a predictable satellite. For Laika was a pioneer, blazing a way where men would follow. Her life was sacrificed on the altar of modern science, already well decorated with willing human sacrifices.

But from the moment Sputnik II spun beyond the earth's atmosphere a race was on, a race that is still being contested and is likely to continue throughout the foreseeable future.

On 1 February 1958 the Americans made another contribution to the International Geophysical Year of 1957-8. They sent up their own artificial satellite, Explorer I, only thirty pounds in weight, a sixth of the weight of Sputnik I, but capable of orbiting throughout a range of two hundred to nearly fourteen hundred miles. Only days later Vanguard I, another US satellite, only six inches in diameter and weighing three and a quarter pounds, was hurled twenty-one hundred miles away from the earth.

The Russians and Americans were racing neck and neck, as it seemed to the surprised spectators of other nations. The race to explore outer space continued steadily from that time onward. Information has been obtained from satellite radio transmitters that has broadened human knowledge on such vitally important subjects for eventual space travellers as gravity changes and magnetic and cosmic ray conditions in the upper ether. Satellites have even dictated back to earth information about infinitesimal particles of matter forming a cosmic dust which are known as micrometeors. Vanguard II, launched a year after Explorer I, was fitted with instruments for radioing back to earth information about high-altitude cloud collected by a scientific weather eye, as it was called.

Space exploration soon divided into two major aims.

The first was to send man aloft in the tracks of the dogs and monkeys first used by the Russians and Americans, so that humans could be trained to space-flight conditions. The second was to hit the moon and demonstrate that the earth's own natural satellite could be reached and perhaps even colonized, for men began to dream of a challenging future.

Moon Probe I, sent up by the Americans in that same momentous year of 1958, exploded after a flight of little more than a minute. Pioneer I also failed to get as far as hoped, but rose to a height of seventy thousand miles.

Pioneer IV rose to within thirty-seven thousand miles of the moon before becoming a tiny planet in outer space.

Lunik I, the Russian moon missile, actually rose to within four thousand miles of the intended target before drifting away to become another tiny planet, but Lunik II hit the moon after a flight lasting thirty-six hours. On impact a Soviet flag unfurled and hung in a truly unearthly atmosphere. This was in the tradition of explorers from the first days when sovereign states had their insignia painted upon a piece of cloth to proclaim that sovereignty.

When Lunik III went sailing out on a carefully calculated orbit that carried the space craft to the far side of the moon, which is not seen from earth, a specially designed camera took photographs of this blind side and after automatic developing they were televised back to waiting Russian stations. If the routine of tradition is not broken Soviet scientists may provide names for craters and mountain ranges on that far side of the moon.

At intervals the Russians and the Americans sent up larger and more technically developed missiles that were actual space craft, like Lunik III, in the sense that they carried equipment capable of performing a calculated task in space.

In May 1960 the Soviet scientists launched a new kind of satellite, larger than any of the others they had fired into the earth's sky, and they claimed that it was indeed a true space craft, but unmanned. At once scientists in other countries took keen notice of the announcement. It could mean only one thing. The Russians would very soon be sending a manned space craft around the earth. In the seventh decade of the twentieth century man was ready to explore the first regions of outer space.

151

The promise made when the Wright brothers demonstrated that man could fly was reaching towards fulfilment.

Eleven months later, in April 1961, the world was electrified by the announcement made over the Soviet radio that a man was actually orbiting the earth in a space craft.

The space craft was Vostok 1, the one-man crew was Yuri Gagarin. He orbited the earth once, covering twenty-six thousand miles in one hour forty-eight minutes, and came down safely inside the Soviet Union.

Less than a month later Alan Shepard, an American, was making a sub-orbital flight in a space craft, Mercury MR-3, covering just under three hundred miles and rising to a height of a hundred and fifteen. He remained fifteen minutes and twenty-two seconds in flight and was brought down safely in the ocean.

The American astronaut Grissom made a comparable space flight two months later, followed by the Soviet cosmonaut Titov who made seventeen orbits of the earth and covered nearly half a million miles in an hour and eighteen minutes longer than a day.

The race was exhilarating. The Russians called their space fliers cosmonauts and brought them down on land, the Americans termed their space men astronauts and brought them down in the Atlantic. To the watching world the difference seemed merely technical.

In February 1962 the American Glenn made three successful orbits of the earth, then in May of the same year another American, Carpenter, duplicated the feat. In August there were marked signs that the Russians were pulling away from their rivals in the space race. For twice in that month of the same year, 1962, Soviet cosmonauts made spectacular flights. Popovich in Vostok IV followed a day after Nikolayev in Vostok III. Nikolayev made sixty-four orbits, Popovich forty-eight, the former travelling more than a million and a half miles, the latter just under a million and a quarter. Single flights of more than a million miles would have seemed incredible just a few years before.

That year of the real Russian break-through was not over before another American astronaut, Shirra, had doubled the orbits successfully made by either of his fellow-countrymen earlier in 1962. That was in October. Seven months later, in

May 1963, the American space craft Mercury MR-9, manned by Cooper, provided by far the best US space performance to date. He remained in flight thirty-four hours to orbit the earth twenty-two times and cover more than half a million miles.

In the following month Tereshkova, another Soviet cosmonaut, in Vostok VI, almost duplicated Popovich's performance of ten months before, making another forty-eight orbits and covering ten thousand miles more than Popovich. It was a performance completely outshone by Bykovsky, in Vostok V, who went into space and orbited two days before Tereshkova, and actually made eighty-one orbits of the earth, remaining in flight only minutes short of five days, during which time he covered two million one hundred and seventy-five thousand miles.

One-manned space craft were beginning to lose their novelty a little. With expectancy the world awaited news of the first multi-manned space craft in flight. Both the Americans and the Russians were known to be pressing ahead with training plans as well as technical developments for space craft with actual crews.

That would be one of the stages before such a scientist's dream as a landing by man on the moon could be achieved. Indeed, there would have to be various important stages of development before the dream could be realized, for not only had men to be landed on the moon, but they had to be brought back to earth safely.

After that the ambition of an enthusiastic space scientist's career need not be limited by a mere dream, for successfully reaching the moon would mean exploration of the earth's satellite, perhaps even the historic routine of colonization.

And after the moon the planets.

Notions that had belonged in the pages of science fiction suddenly assumed the shape of future possibilities. Man was on the point of preparing himself to explore the universe of which he was the inhabitant of a smaller planet in a single solar system.

Another break-through was awaited.

More than a year passed after Bykovsky and Tereshkova had made their space flights in June 1963. Then came the announcement of absorbing interest that a new-type Soviet space craft had been launched. This was Voskhod I. It was manned by three cosmonauts, Komarov, Feoktistov, and Yegorov.

On 12 October 1964 they were shot into space and made sixteen orbits of the earth in their multi-manned space craft, which remained in flight for seventeen minutes longer than a day, and covered almost half a million miles, before it was brought down and the cosmonaut team released from their capsule.

When the three cosmonauts stepped out on *terra firma* the Soviet record to that time was impressive. Nine of their cosmonauts had jointly spent more than four hundred hours in space flight. The distance in space they had covered was more than seven million miles. That was the equivalent of fourteen return trips to the moon.

The Americans were known to be forging ahead with the preparation of a two-man Gemini space craft, and the world knew that, despite the Russian's lead at the end of 1964, the race was still on. But certain conceptions had automatically changed with the successful launching of Voskhod 1. It was now possible to send different types of trained cosmonauts and astronauts into space. One man could be the pilot, another a scientist, a third a doctor. Moreover, a significant advance could be made by freeing space craft crew members from the restrictions of pressure suits.

At Fort Worth the Americans continued with basic experiments such as a possible soft landing for their new Gemini space craft, which was more than twice as heavy as the Mercury range of space craft. This would be a parachute-aided landing of the capsule on dry land. Veteran astronauts like Virgil Grissom took their seats at the controls of the Gemini Procedures Trainer, which readied American astronauts for eventual multi-manned flight. New names were announced. Major James McDivitt and Major Edward White were mentioned as the likely American team to man the first Gemini space craft, which would be launched in the first half of 1965, another year with a fresh break-through in space flight techniques.

Again the Russians edged in front.

In March 1965 Voskhod II was launched, with a two-man crew, Lieutenant-Colonel Alexei Leonov and his co-cosmonaut Pavel Belyaev. They remained in flight for twenty-six hours, slightly longer than Voshkod I, and made seventeen orbits against their predecessor's sixteen. But the flight of Voskhod II was marked

154

. . . had plans for Major Edward White to leave his space craft and float about twenty-five feet from it

155

by what seemed to earth-bound viewers later watching their television screens as a near-miracle. On that momentous 18 March, Alexei Leonov actually got out of the space craft and when the Soviet film was released, was seen by millions of viewers to float in outer space, attached to his satellite home by a slender cord, which was, as it proved, merely a precaution.

A couple of months later, in May 1965, after they had thoroughly examined photographic and other records of that thrilling flight, in which man actually left his craft to take the first steps of an independent personal exploration of space, Russian scientists issued fuller reports. Their findings were given by Dr Oleg Gazenko, a Soviet expert on space medicine, to a gathering of two hundred of two hundred scientists in Chicago.

His audience were shown a film that ran for nearly half an hour. Some of it was in colour, other television camera shots were in back and white. The film record actually showed Leonov closing one eye on a command given him from earth while spinning in space. The curvature of the earth was visible to the audience through one of the space craft's portholes.

The big moment was when Leonov left the craft. He was shown with his hands outstretched, his legs apart, a short distance from Voskhod II.

Dr Gazenko explained that the cosmonaut had a genuine space problem 'in orienting himself when he turned his eyes away from the space ship.' In short, as soon as Leonov removed his gaze from something fixed in relation to himself and his own space velocity, his space-time judgement was impaired. Or, as Dr Gazenko put it, ' His orientation in space was disturbed and the direction of the space ship was very hard to find.'

The real miracle was that Alexei Leonov was able to adjust his mind and senses to this impairment, so that it was only temporary.

But that historic brief personal exploration of space by a man outside a space craft pointed to problems that would have to be solved before men could venture from a landed moon craft. Perhaps the problems would terminate what had been the most momentous race in history.

The very fact that Dr Gazenko was in Chicago, finding common ground with American scientists, augured well for the discovery of an even greater area of common ground where ideas and knowledge could be shared for the benefit of all mankind. For there had been reports, only three weeks before Dr Gazenko's Chicago lecture, that Soviet radio-astronomers might have discovered evidence of another civilization existing millions of miles away in space.

The possibility had to be faced squarely that man might have neighbours somewhere in space.

Meanwhile the Americans pushed ahead with their own plans for making 1965 the most significant year to date in the space race.

On 3 June McDivitt and White were blasted off on a Titan rocket at Cape Kennedy, Florida, and their Gemini space craft was hurled into orbital flight. They had plans to rendezvous with their Titan booster rocket, but the attempt was called off because of the risk of using up too much precious fuel. So their other plan for Major White to leave Gemini iv, was put into operation. Actually White delayed stepping into space until the space craft was making its third orbit. Then he stood up and said, ' It's a most relaxed period.' A few seconds later he was outside the capsule and either swimming or walking in space.

He was a hundred and fifty miles above the Pacific Ocean and connected to Gemini iv by a gold-plated cord twenty-five feet in length. In his hand he held a space gun by means of which he propelled himself around.

He remained outside the space craft for fourteen minutes, four more than Alexei Leonov. In that time he travelled at a speed of 17,500 miles an hour, and with Gemini iv crossed over Mexico, the South-west United States, the Gulf of Mexico, Florida, and the Atlantic coast of the USA.

That same evening a Soviet commentator appeared on Moscow's television and announced, ' The Soviet people sincerely congratulate the two cosmonauts and the American scientists on this achievement.'

Four days later, after completing sixty-two orbits, James McDivitt and Edward White splashed down in the Atlantic, four hundred miles from Bermuda and less than fifty from the aircraft carrier *Wasp*. Their space mission had lasted three minutes under ninety-eight hours. Dr Joseph Shea, director of the National Aeronautical and Space Administration's Apollo moon project, was reported as saying in New York a few hours afterwards that

McDivitt and White's historic flight ' will certainly shorten the road to the moon '.

Three and a half months later, in late September, Commander Scott Carpenter, an American pioneer astronaut, rose from the bed of the Pacific after living at a depth of two hundred and five feet for no less than twenty-nine days and fourteen hours. He had spent twice as long under water as any man previously. For practically a month he had inhabited, on the ocean's bed, a special steel capsule measuring fifty-eight feet by twelve. When he rose again into the earth's atmosphere off La Jolla, California, he had much valuable scientific data.

Aquanauts, it appeared, were as capable of making history as astronauts, and as capable of furthering man's store of knowledge about the elements fashioning his mortal home.

Less than three months later the astronauts again made history, when the American headed past the Russians in the space race. On 18 December 1965, Commander James Lovell and Lieutenant-Colonel Frank Borman splashed down in a copybook landing less than nine miles from the carrier *Wasp*. They had completed a fabulous fortnight in space.

In their record fourteen-day space mission they had orbited the earth some two hundred and six times and had travelled through five million one hundred and twenty-nine thousand miles.

Moreover, for the first time, on that great flight a space rendezvous had been kept with another space craft. Lovell and Borman had travelled in Gemini VII. On 15 December, some hundred and eighty-five miles above the Mariana Islands, in the Pacific, they joined in orbital flight at 17,500 miles an hour Gemini VI, in which were Captain Walter Schirra and Major Thomas Stafford.

Gemini VI had been launched ten minutes less than six hours previously.

The actual moment of the orbital rendezvous was 7.27 Greenwich Mean Time.

When Gemini VI arrived in orbit it was twelve hundred miles from Gemini VII. For a chase of a hundred and three thousand miles the two space crews worked to close that mighty gap until they were within one foot of each other. On earth one of the astronaut quartet was heard to shout, ' We did it !'

President Lyndon Johnson's comment on the success of the complicated orbital manoeuvring echoed the words of Dr Shea. The President said the two space crews had moved man ' one step higher on the stairway to the moon '.

The old year of 1965 had only one day left when Captain Schirra told a Press conference in Houston, Texas, ' We got within a foot, but we had agreed before the flight that the space craft would not touch.'

It seemed the astronauts were becoming almost casual about their challenging missions!

To the enthralled spectators of other nations, already enjoying the advantages provided by communications satellites such as Telstar and Early Bird, the Space Age had really arrived. Both the Russians and the Americans had attained a spatial proficiency that released men from earth-fired space craft to be ready to employ their human senses in exploring a realm in which man was still a stranger.

Man was, in effect, about to emulate his own earlier conception of a god.

Only the future could show whether man was big enough to wear the mantle of his own greatness.